The Oven

by Sophie Goldstein

For Mike!
thanks for all
the amazing
work you do
@ meals on wheels

♡ sophie G!

The Oven
Published by AdHouse Books

Content is © copyright 2015 Sophie Goldstein.
www.redinkradio.com
AdHouse logo is © copyright 2015 AdHouse Books.

AdHouse Books
ISBN 1-935233-33-5
ISBN 978-1-935233-33-6
10 9 8 7 6 5 4 3 2 1

Design: Goldstein + Pitzer

AdHouse Books
3905 Brook Road
Richmond, VA 23227 USA
www.adhousebooks.com

First Printing, April 2015

Printed in China

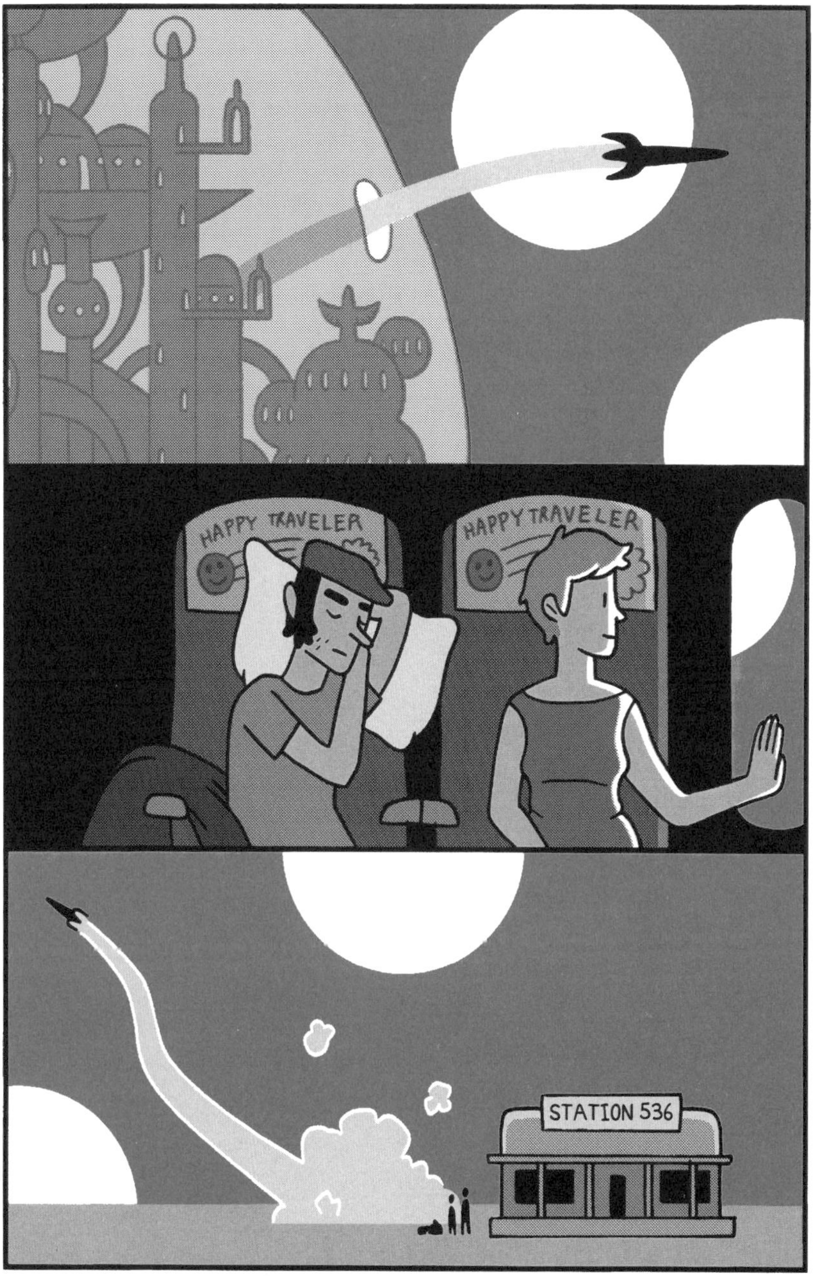
HAPPY TRAVELER
HAPPY TRAVELER
STATION 536

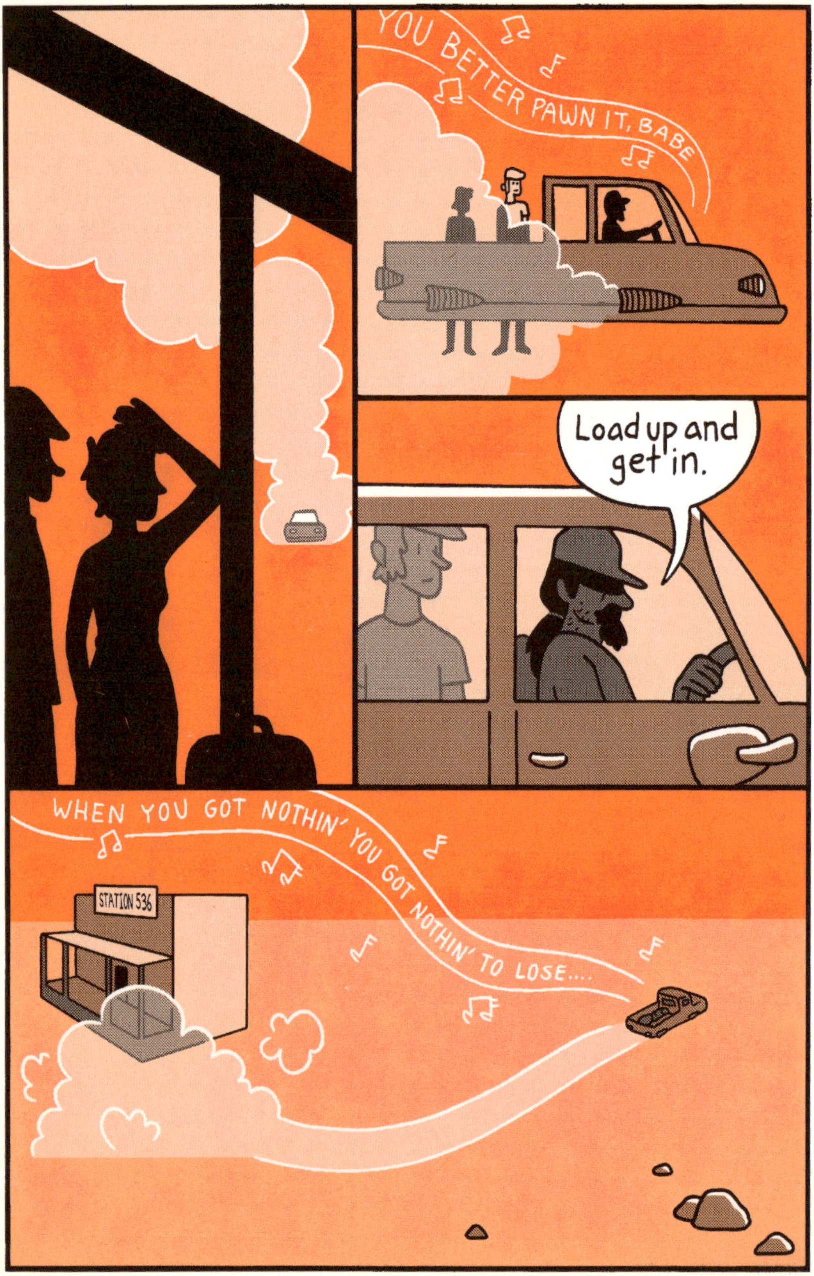
YOU BETTER PAWN IT, BABE
Load up and get in.
WHEN YOU GOT NOTHIN' YOU GOT NOTHIN' TO LOSE....
STATION 536

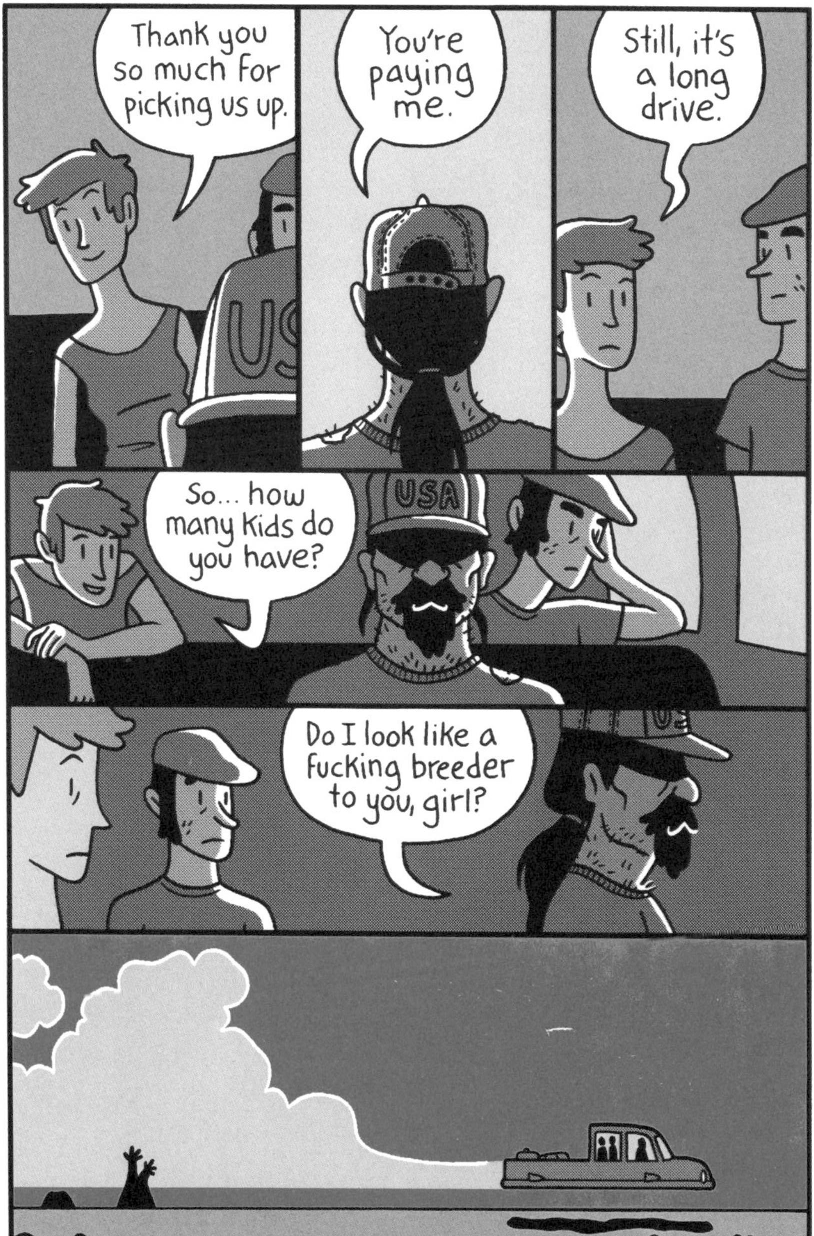
Thank you so much for picking us up.
You're paying me.
Still, it's a long drive.
So... how many kids do you have?
Do I look like a fucking breeder to you, girl?

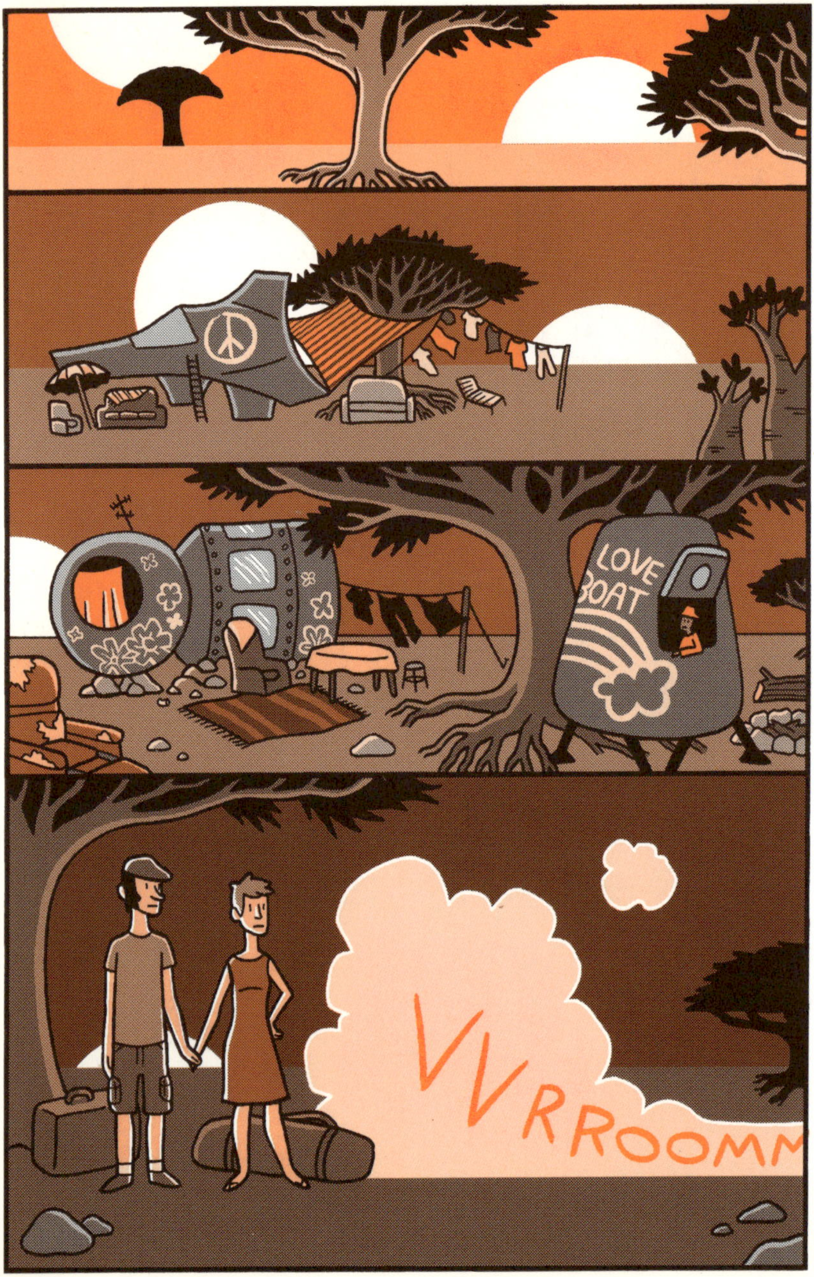
LOVE
BOAT
VVRROOMM

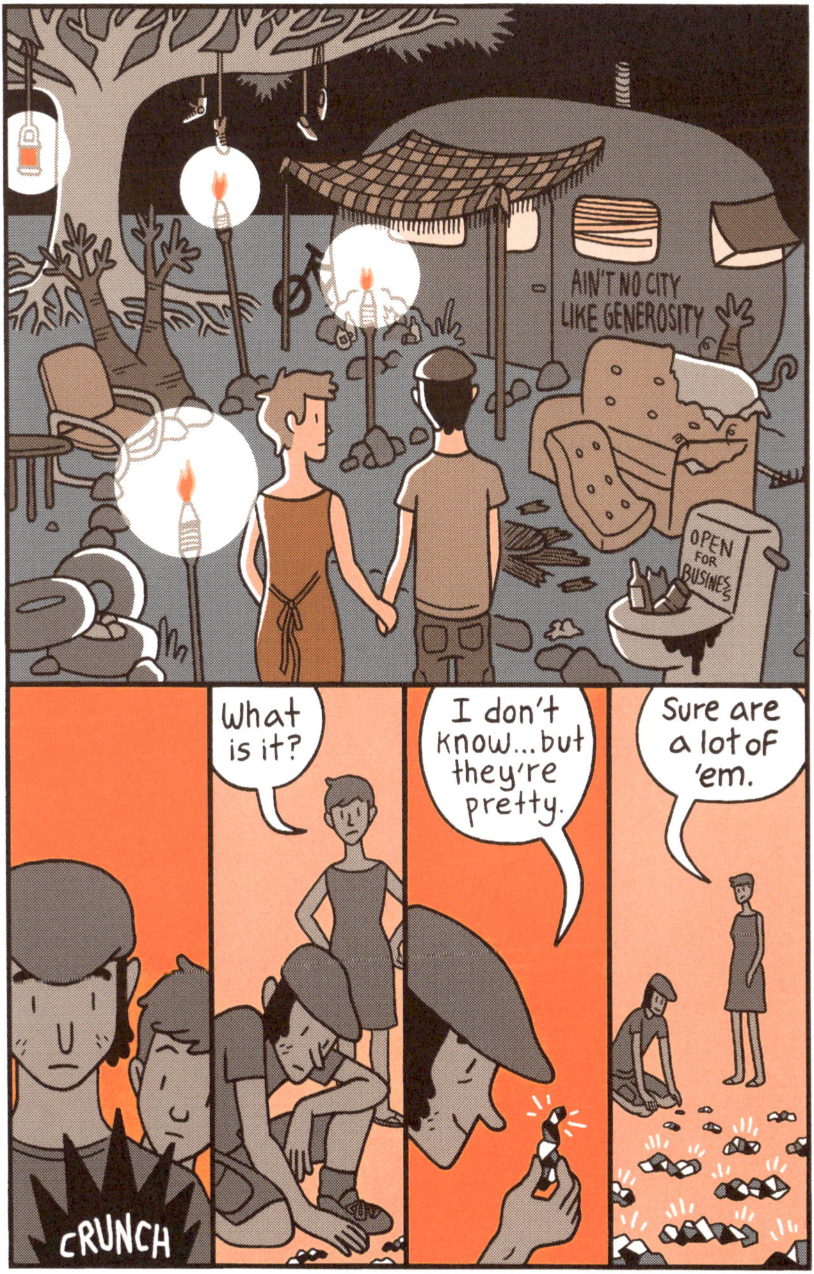
AIN'T NO CITY
LIKE GENEROSITY
OPEN FOR BUSINESS
CRUNCH
What is it?
I don't know... but they're pretty.
Sure are a lot of 'em.

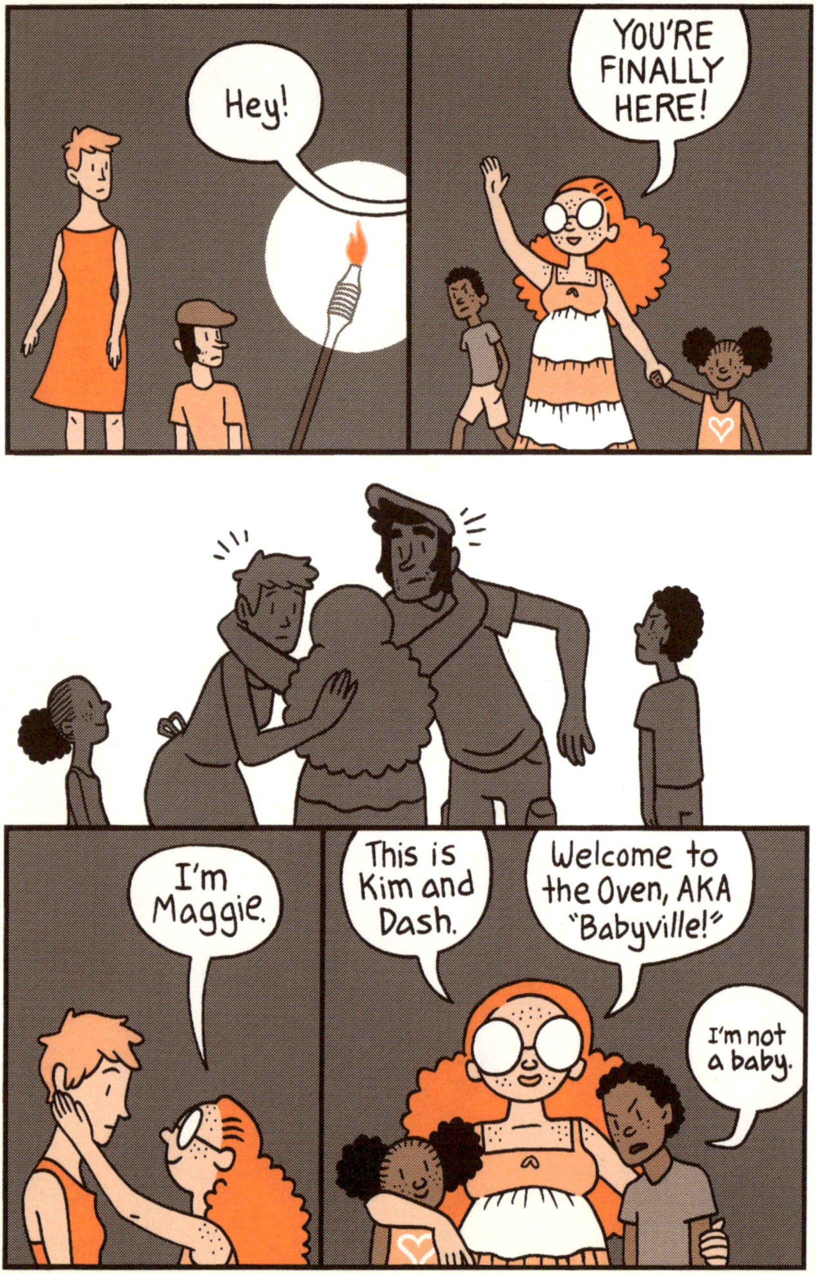
Hey!
YOU'RE FINALLY HERE!
I'm Maggie.
This is Kim and Dash.
Welcome to the Oven, AKA "Babyville!"
I'm not a baby.

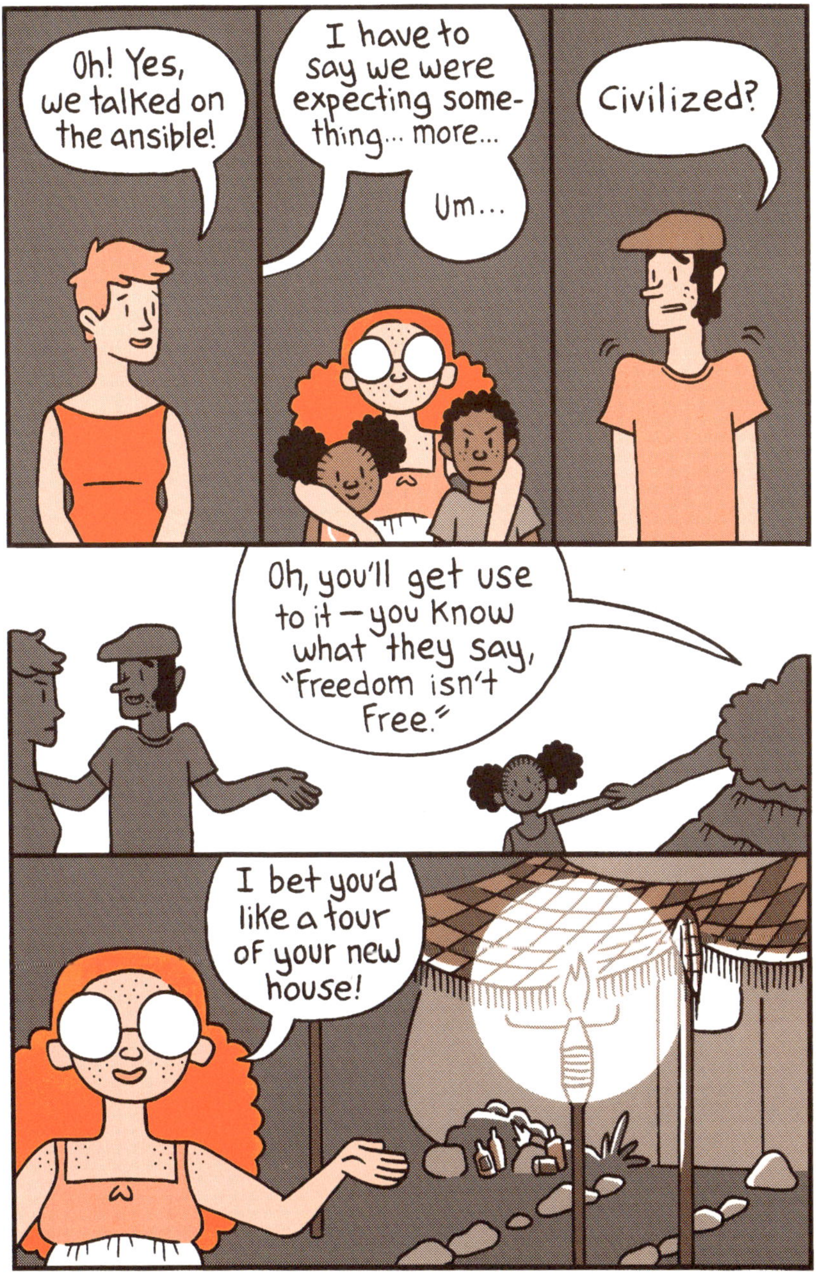
Oh! Yes, we talked on the ansible!
I have to say we were expecting some-thing... more...
Um...
Civilized?
Oh, you'll get use to it—you know what they say, "Freedom isn't Free."
I bet you'd like a tour of your new house!

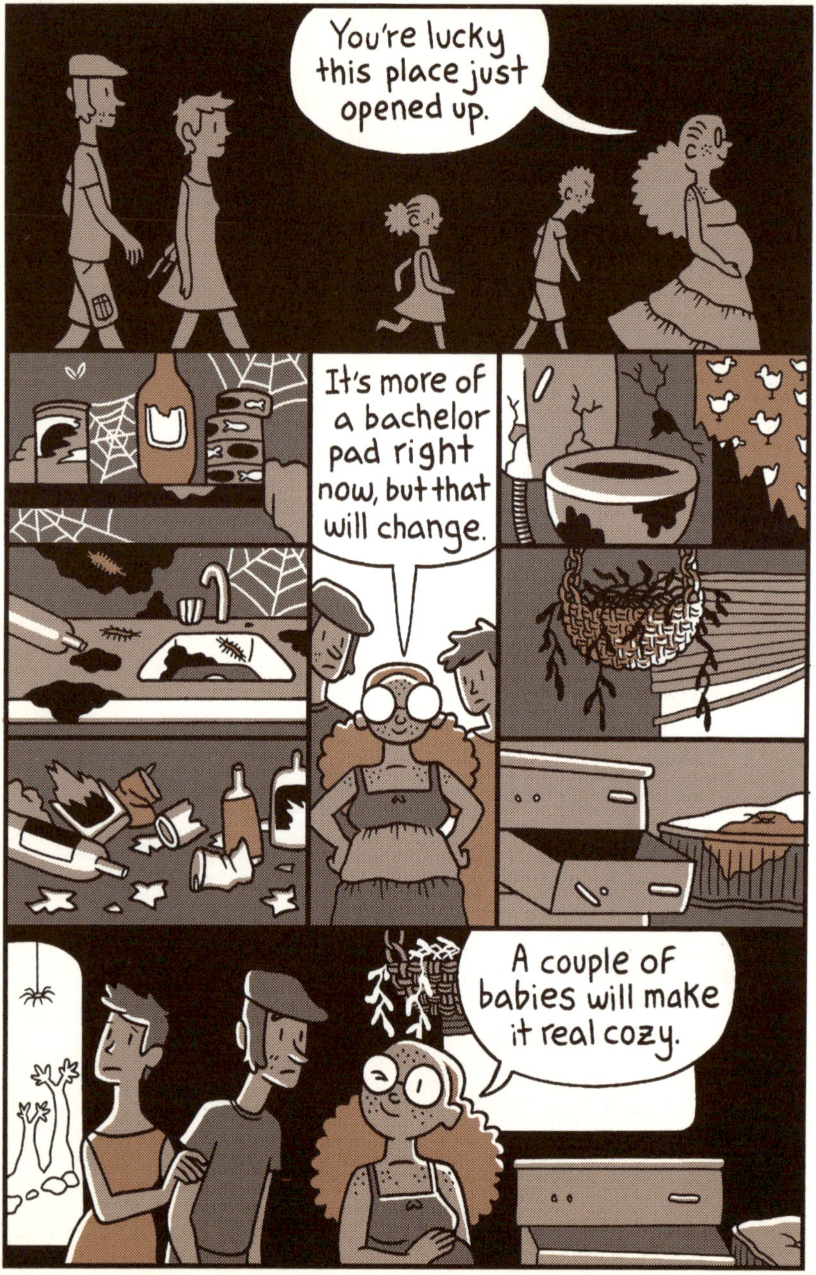
You're lucky this place just opened up.
It's more of a bachelor pad right now, but that will change.
A couple of babies will make it real cozy.

Thank you for arranging all this.
I'm just happy to have the company.
There aren't as many families around here as I'd like.
But I thought that was the whole idea of this place.
With more people like you, one day it will be.
Mom?
That's my name! See you soon, guys.

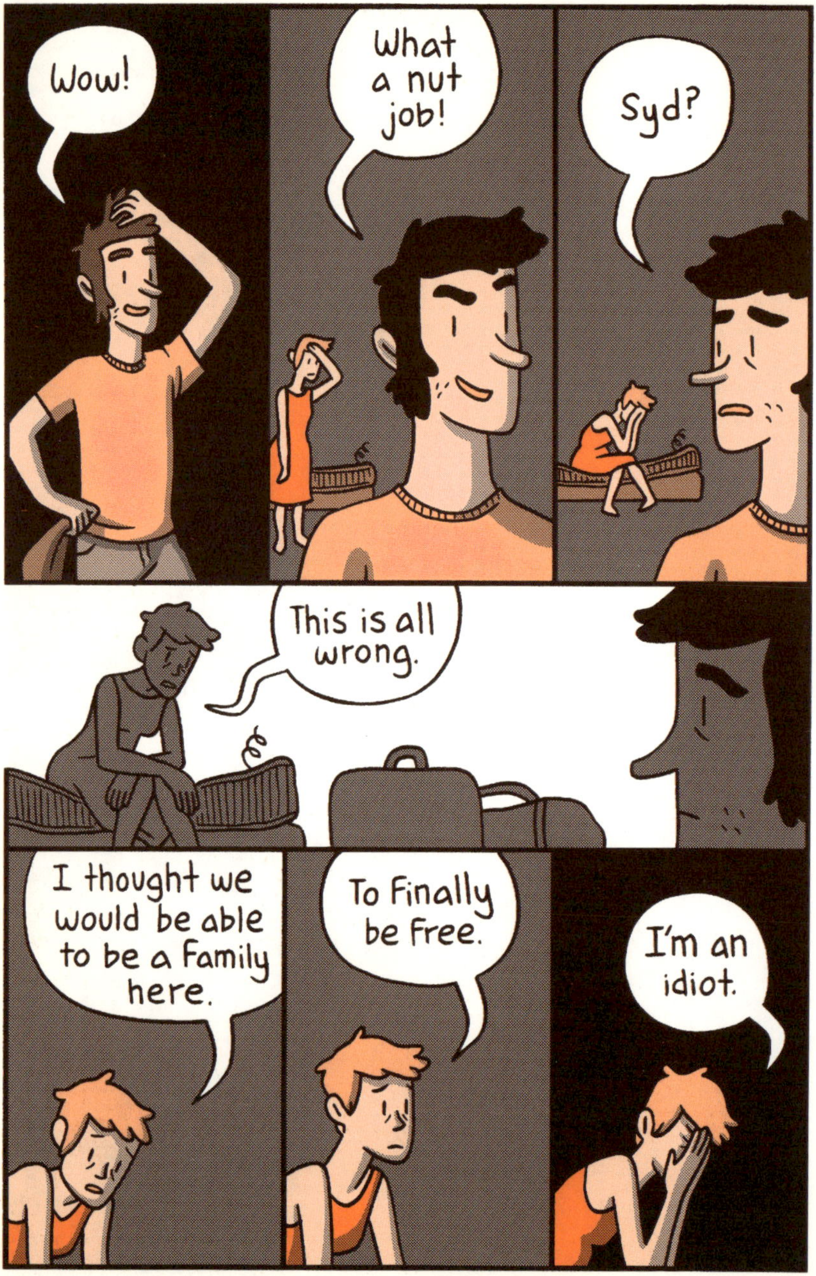
Wow!
What a nut job!
Syd?
This is all wrong.
I thought we would be able to be a family here.
To finally be free.
I'm an idiot.

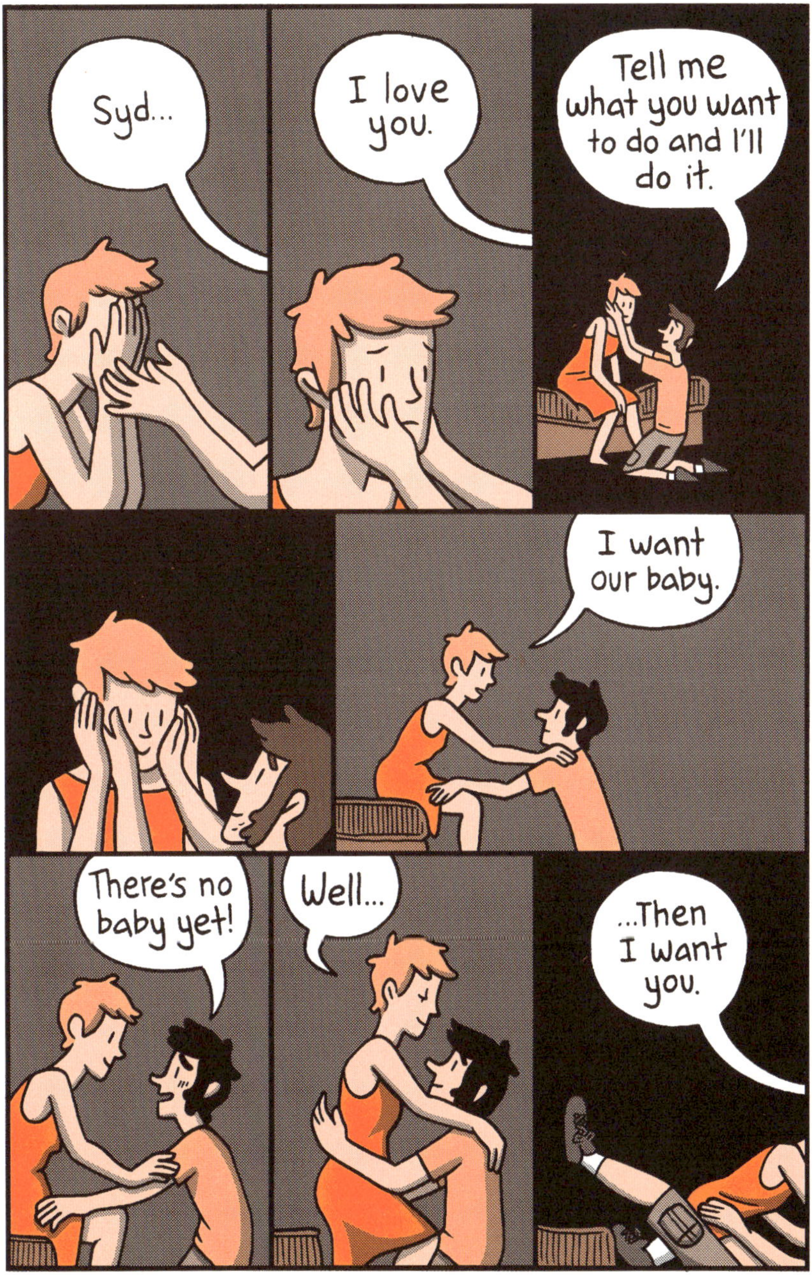
Syd...
I love you.
Tell me what you want to do and I'll do it.
I want our baby.
There's no baby yet!
Well...
...Then I want you.

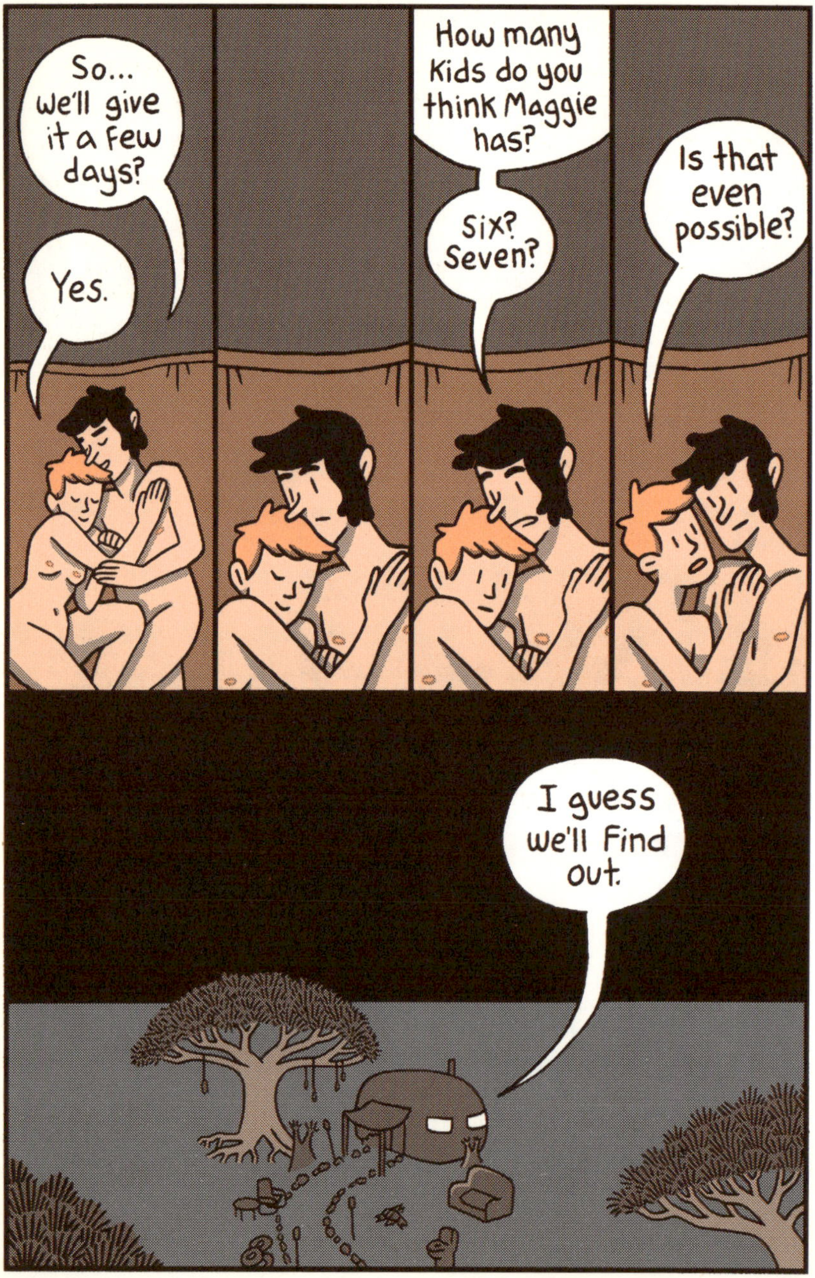
So... we'll give it a few days?
Yes.
How many kids do you think Maggie has?
Six? Seven?
Is that even possible?
I guess we'll find out.

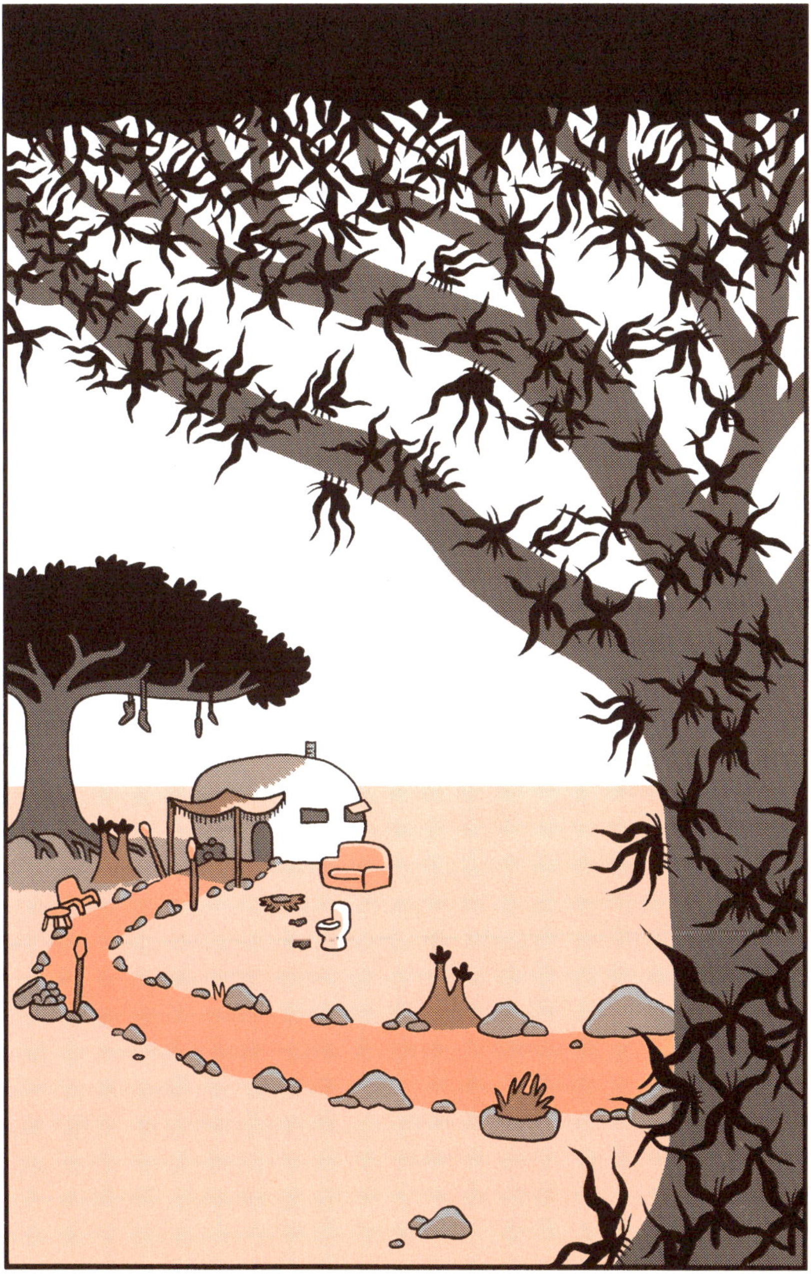

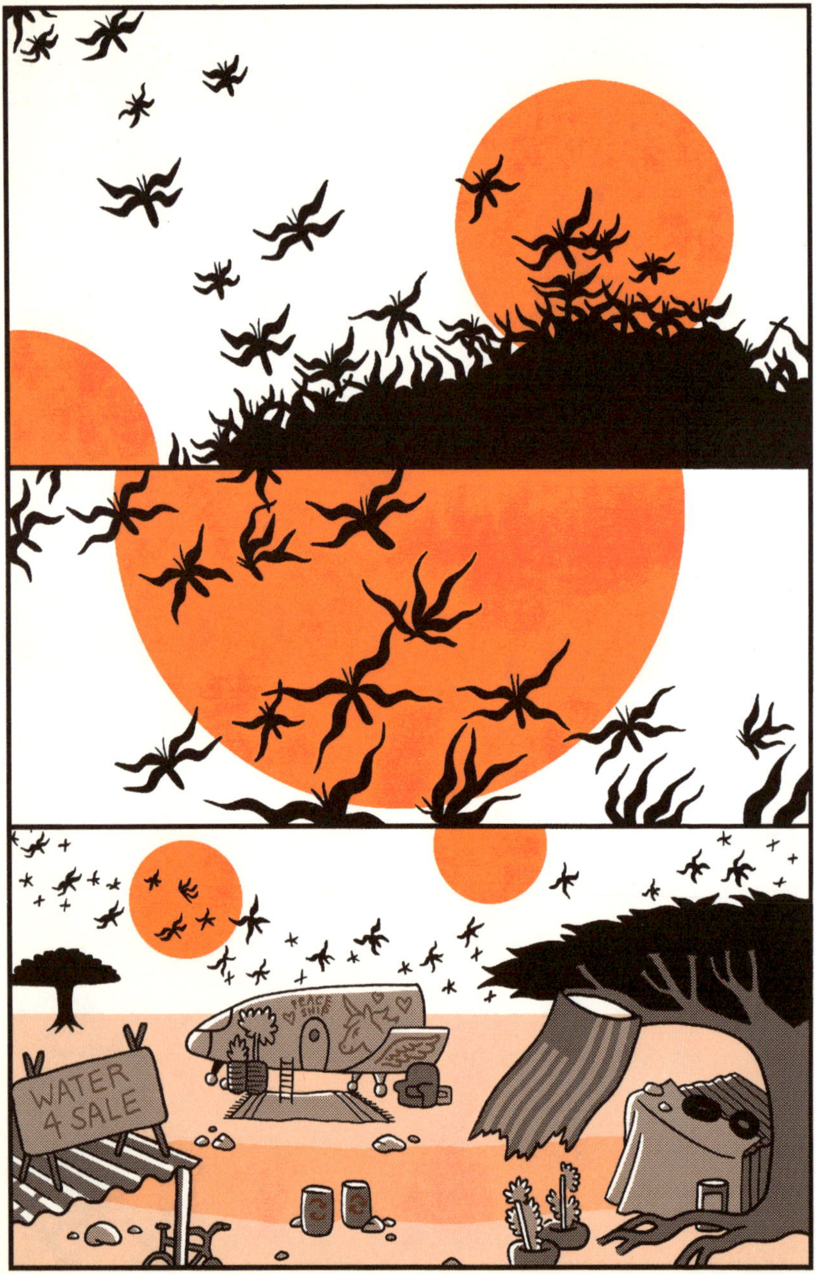
PEACE SHIP
WATER 4 SALE

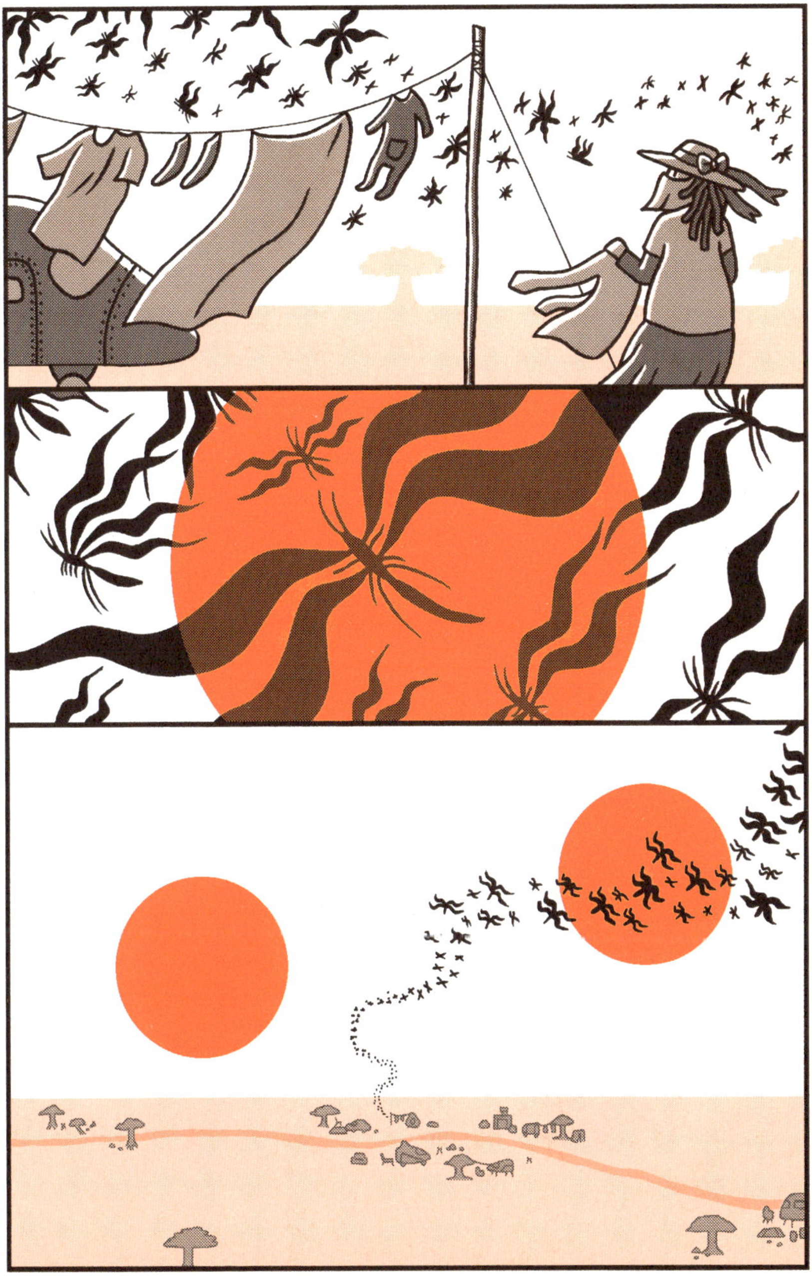

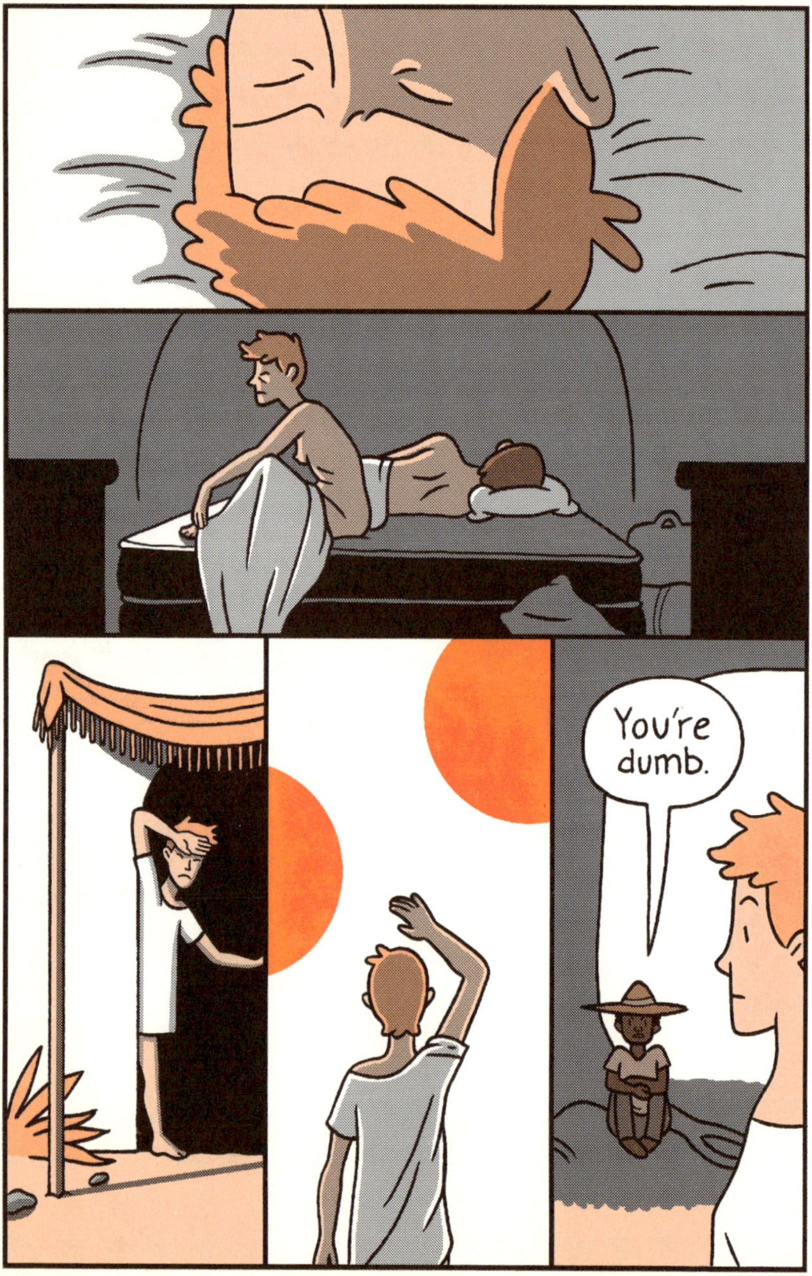
You're dumb.

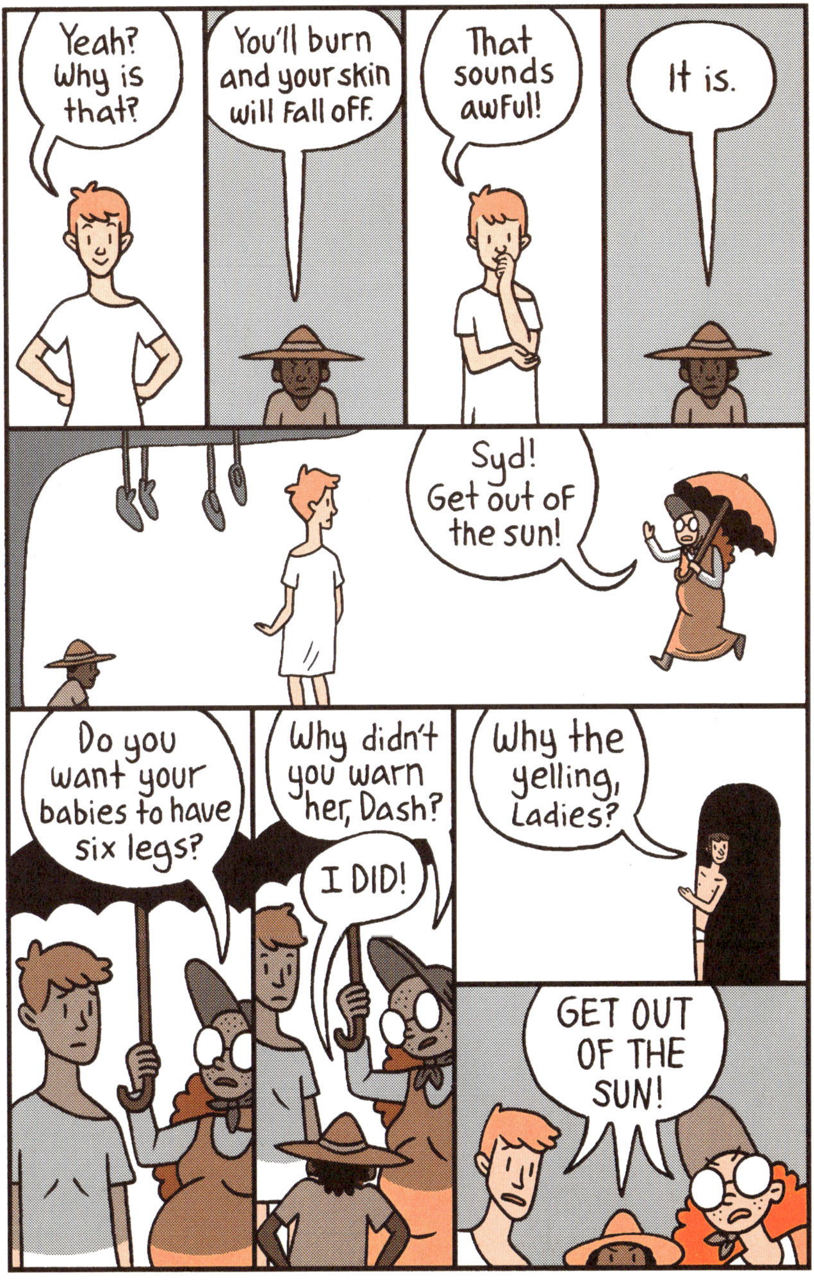
Yeah? Why is that?
You'll burn and your skin will fall off.
That sounds awful!
It is.
Syd! Get out of the sun!
Do you want your babies to have six legs?
Why didn't you warn her, Dash?
I DID!
Why the yelling, Ladies?
GET OUT OF THE SUN!

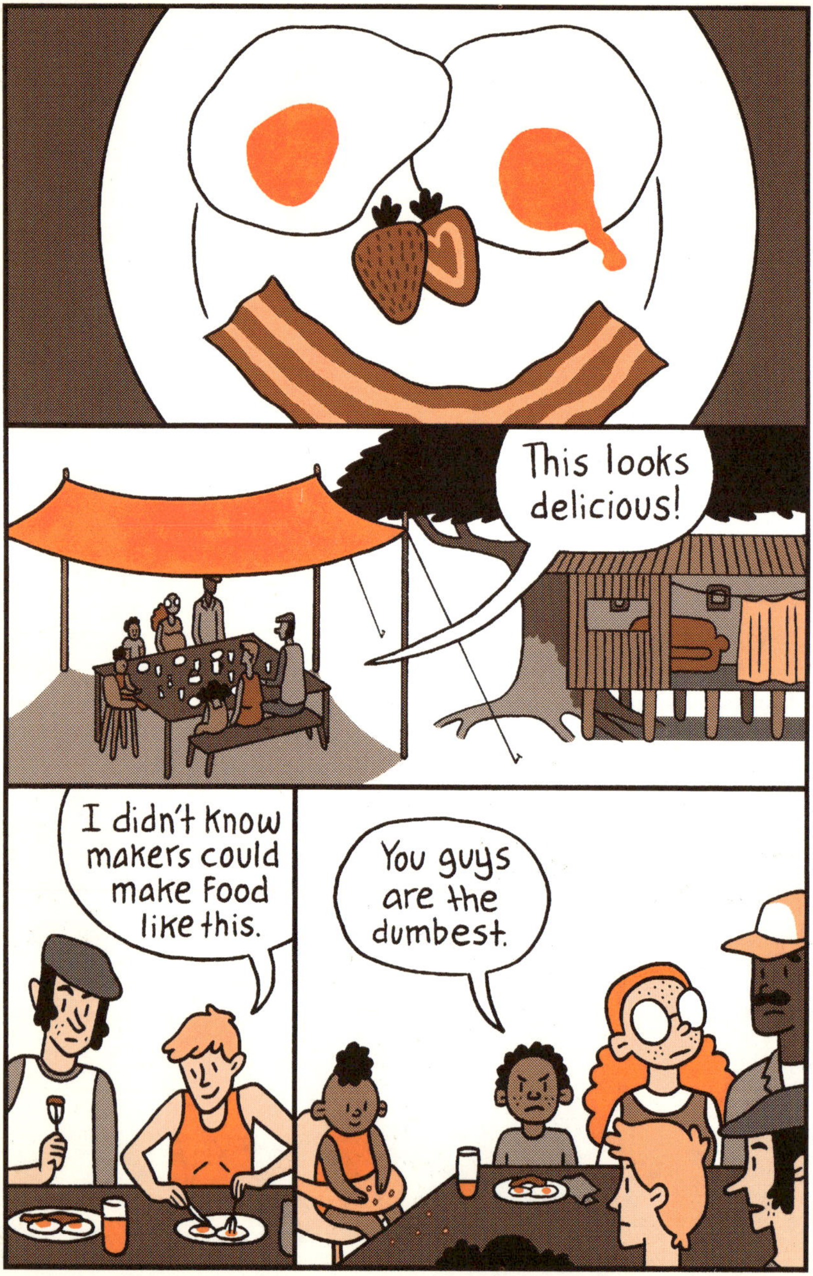
This looks delicious!
I didn't know makers could make food like this.
You guys are the dumbest.

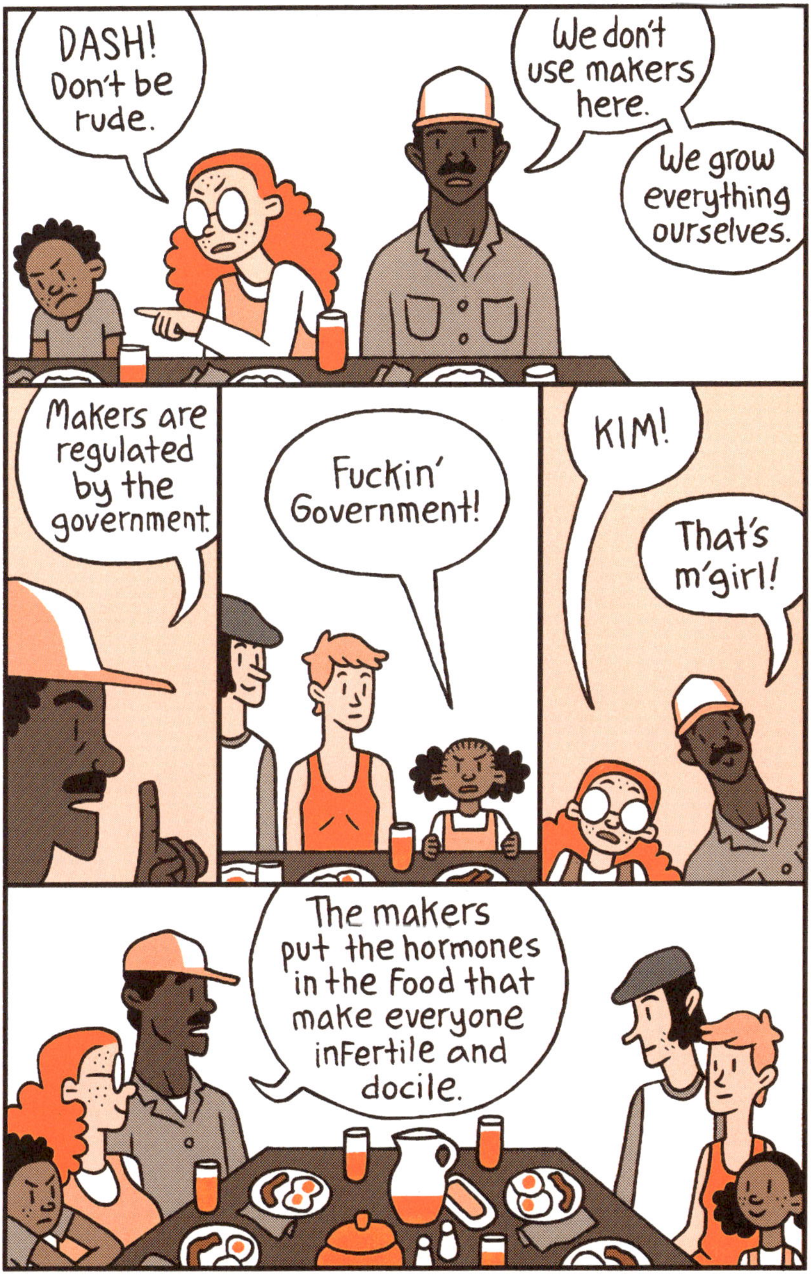
DASH! Don't be rude.
We don't use makers here.
We grow everything ourselves.
Makers are regulated by the government.
Fuckin' Government!
KIM!
That's m'girl!
The makers put the hormones in the food that make everyone infertile and docile.

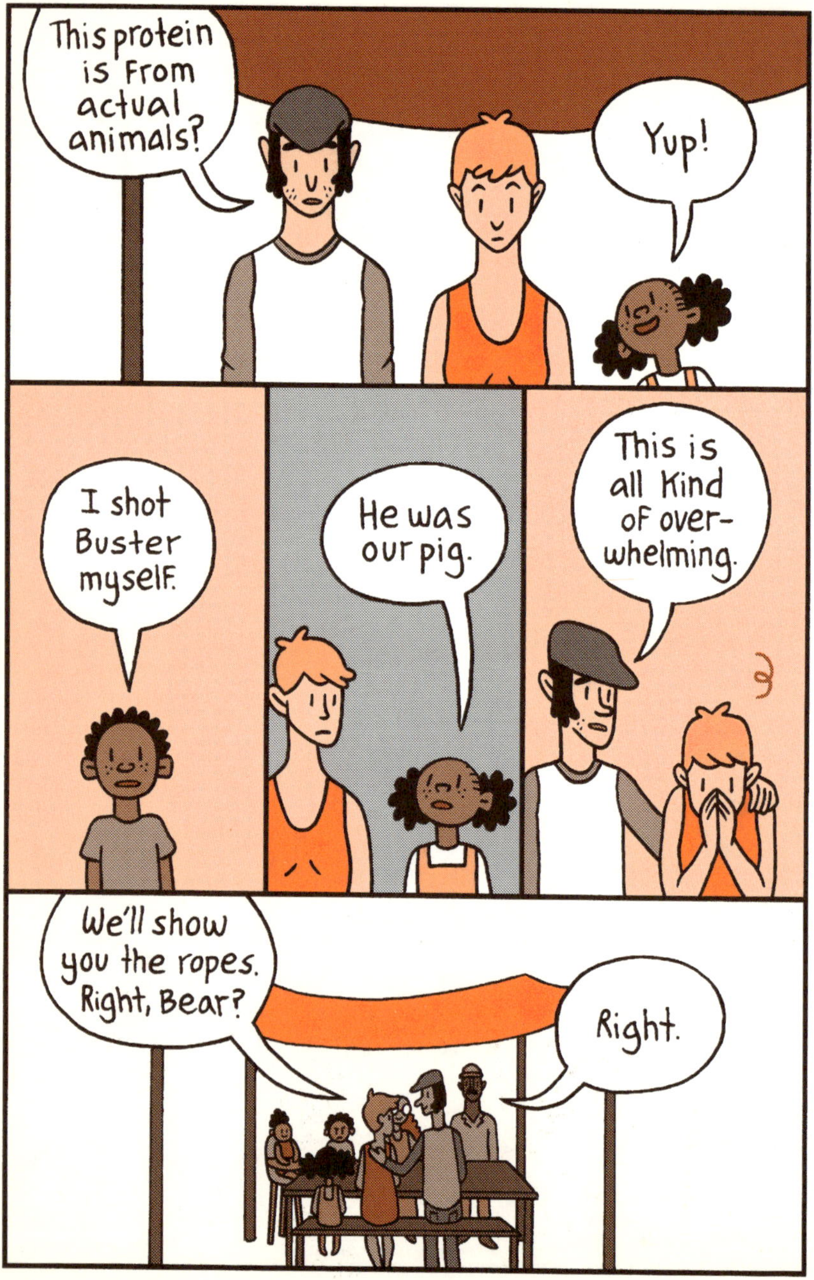
This protein is from actual animals?
Yup!
I shot Buster myself.
He was our pig.
This is all kind of over-whelming.
We'll show you the ropes. Right, Bear?
Right.

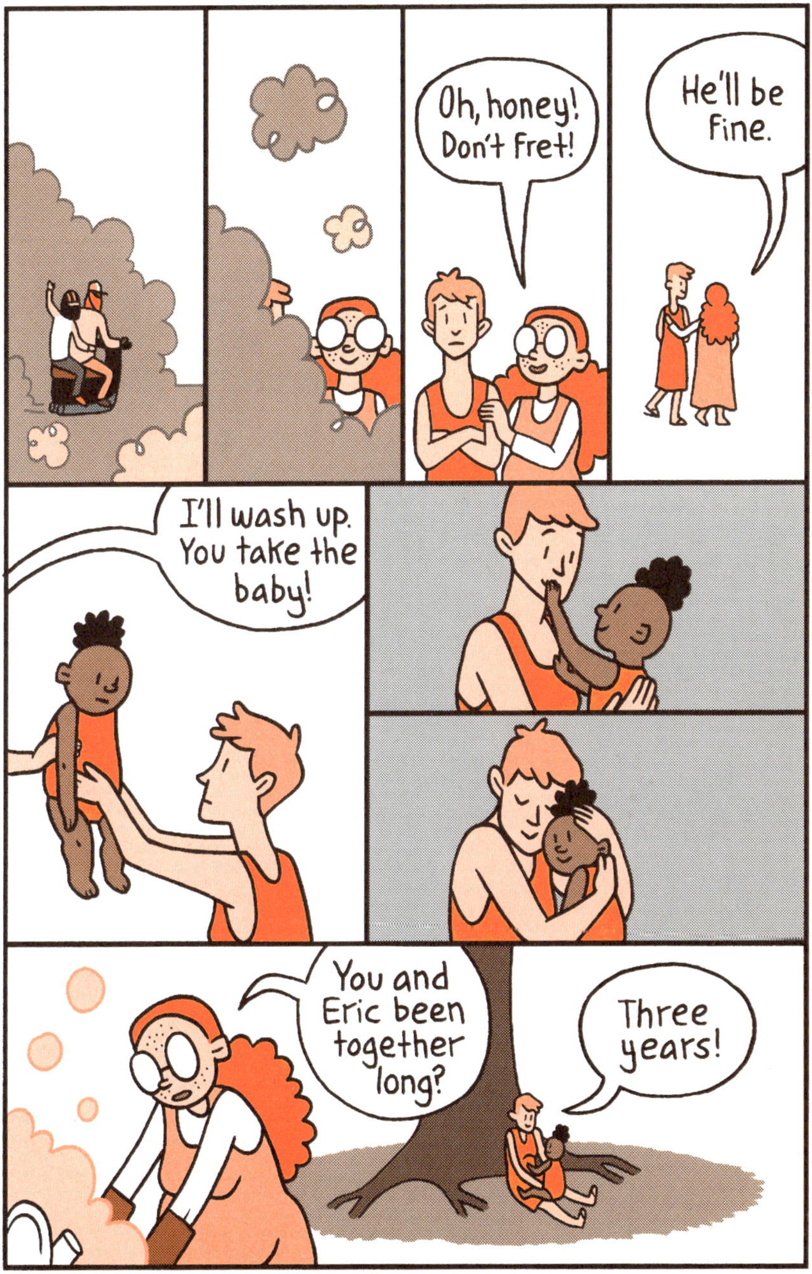
Oh, honey! Don't fret!
He'll be fine.
I'll wash up. You take the baby!
You and Eric been together long?
Three years!

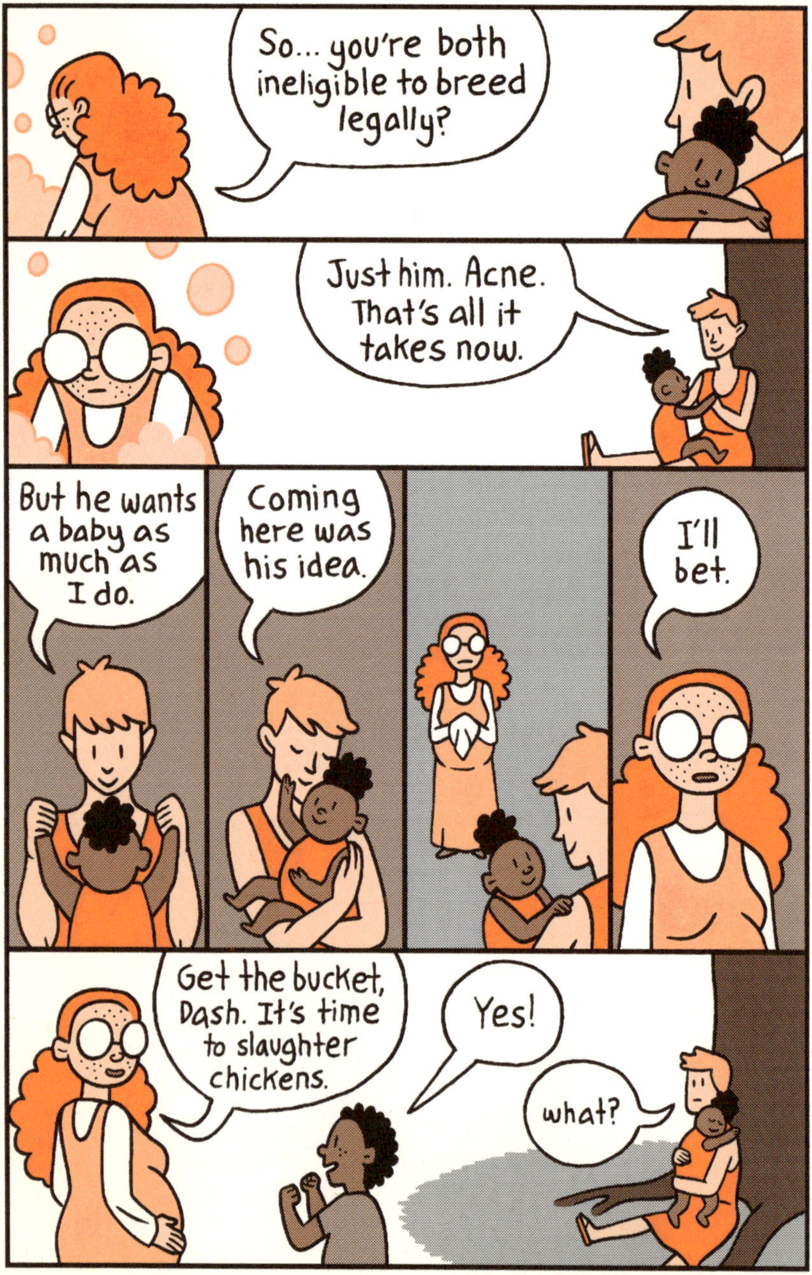
So... you're both ineligible to breed legally?
Just him. Acne. That's all it takes now.
But he wants a baby as much as I do.
Coming here was his idea.
I'll bet.
Get the bucket, Dash. It's time to slaughter chickens.
Yes!
what?

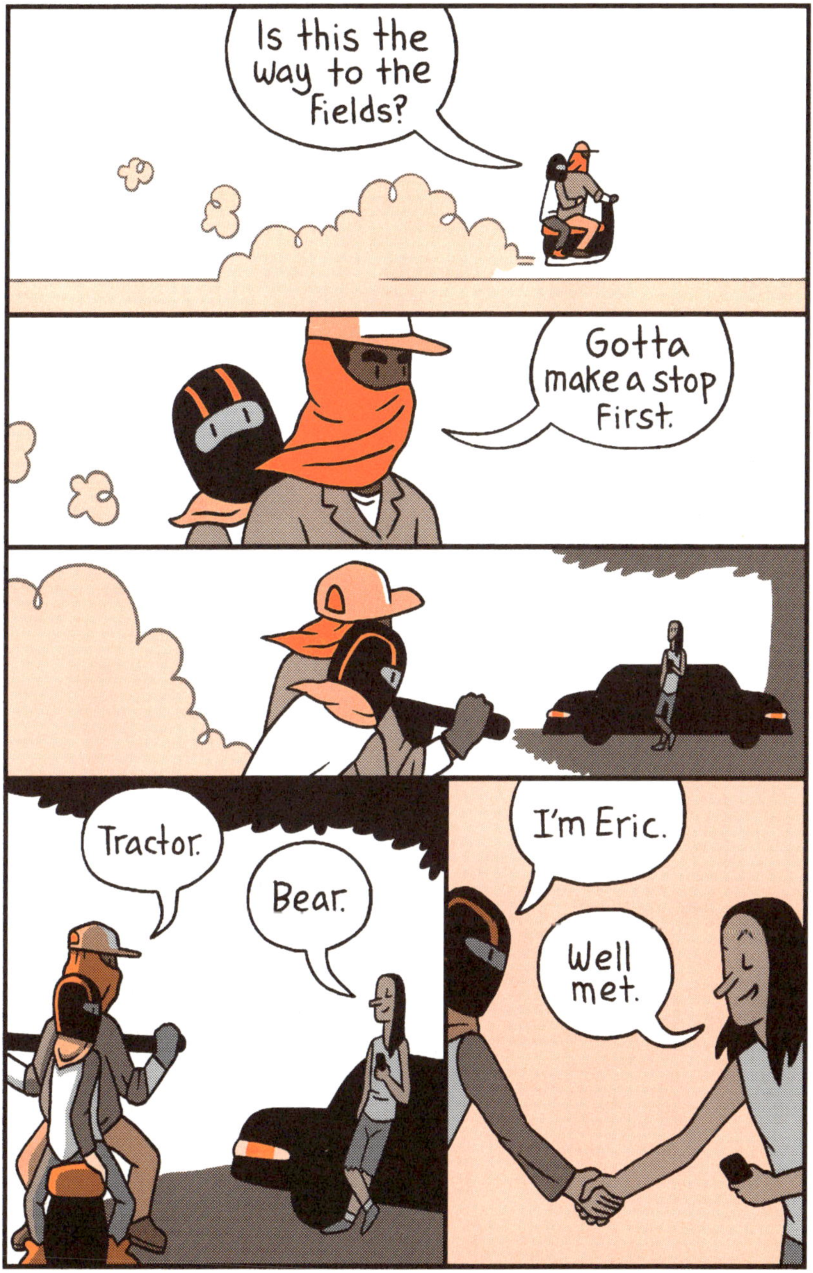
Is this the way to the fields?
Gotta make a stop first.
Tractor.
Bear.
I'm Eric.
Well met.

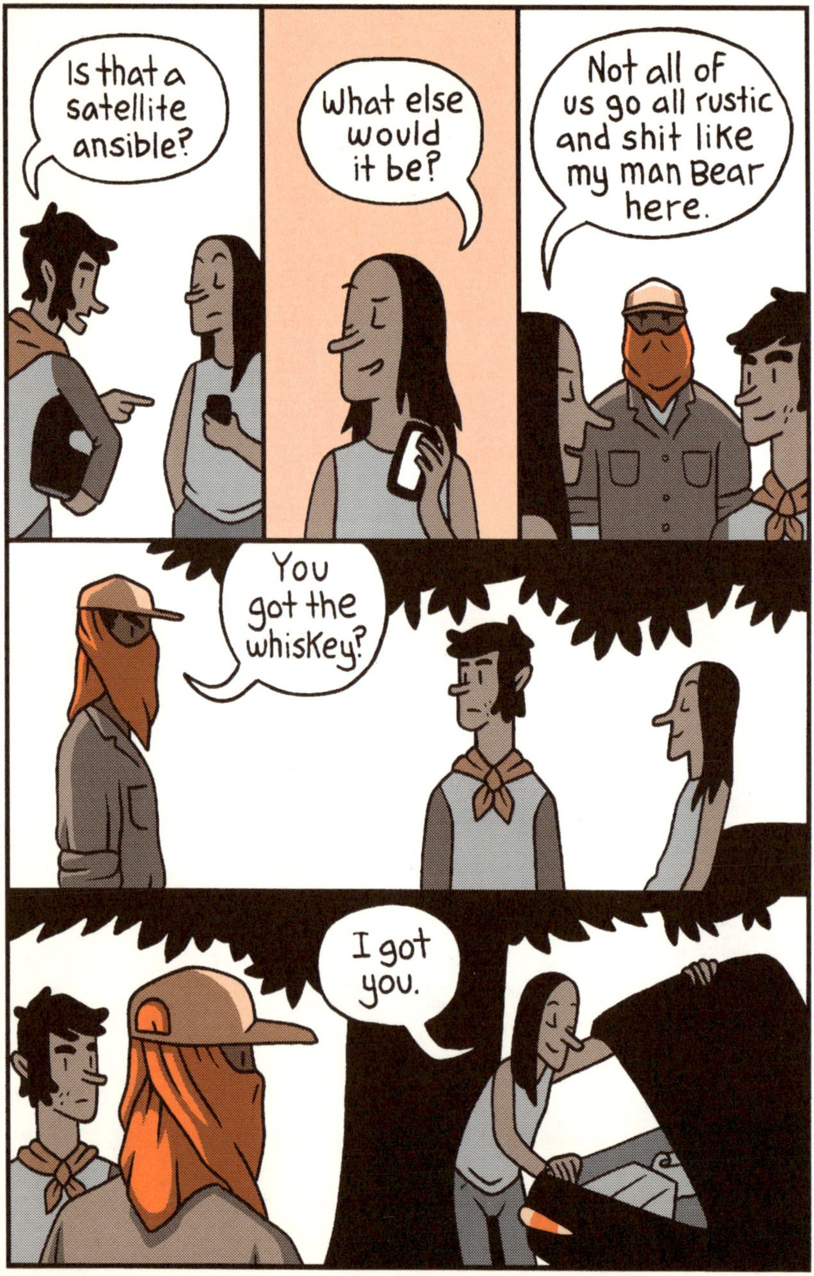
Is that a satellite ansible?
What else would it be?
Not all of us go all rustic and shit like my man Bear here.
You got the whiskey?
I got you.

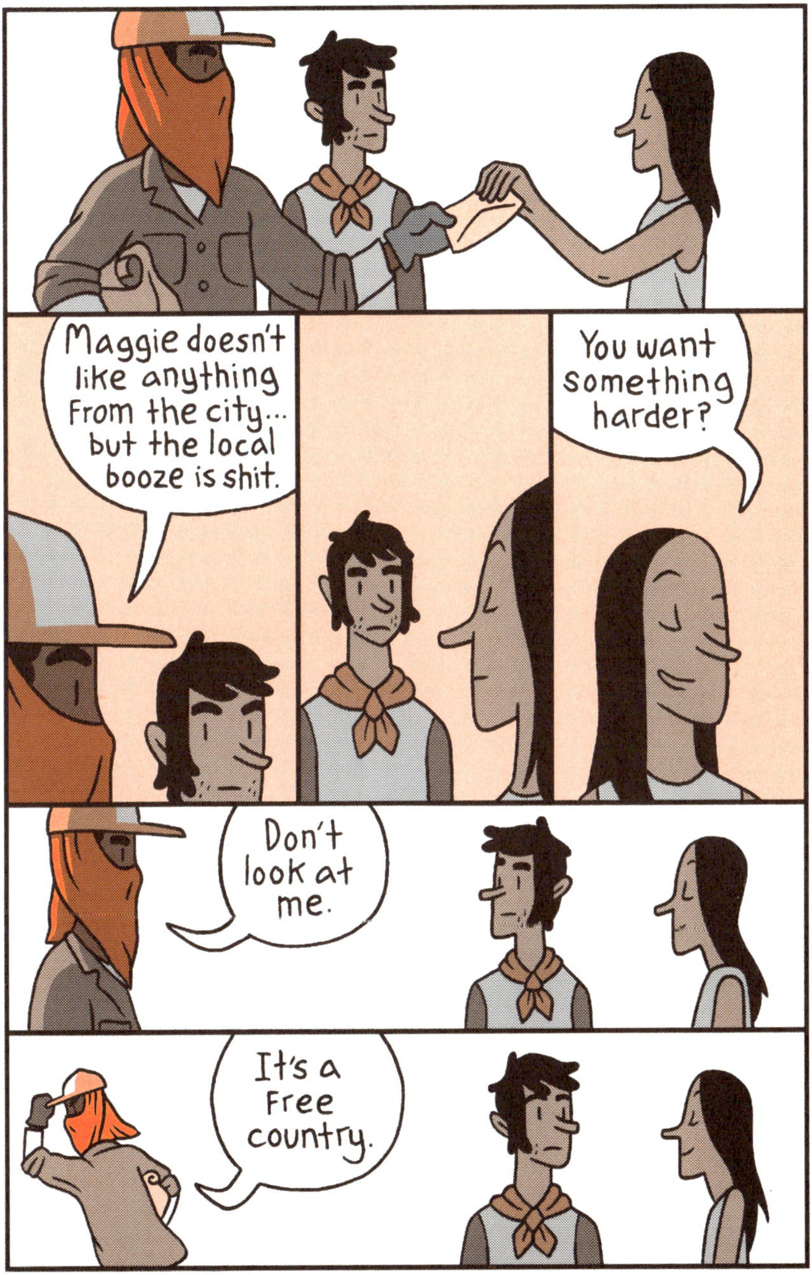
Maggie doesn't like anything from the city... but the local booze is shit.
You want something harder?
Don't look at me.
It's a free country.

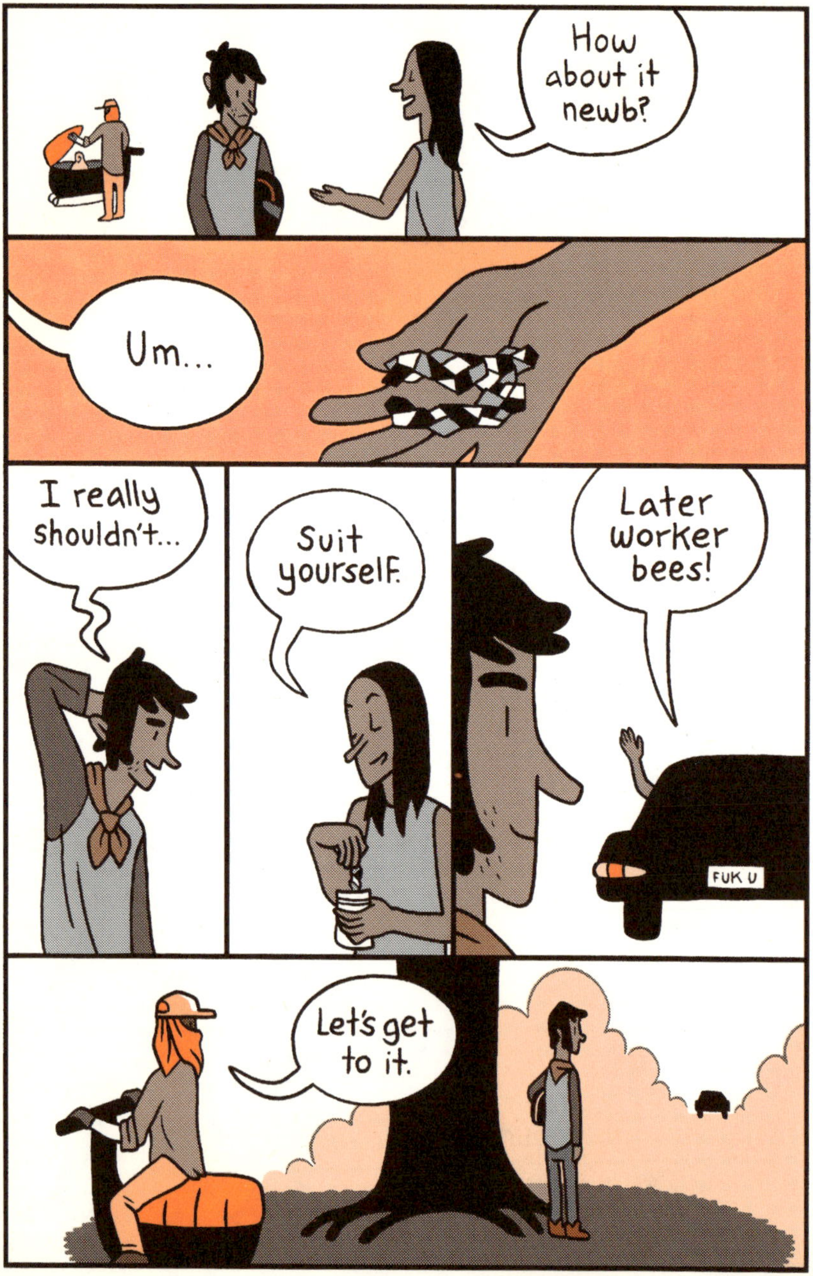
How about it newb?
Um...
I really shouldn't...
Suit yourself.
Later worker bees!
FUK U
Let's get to it.

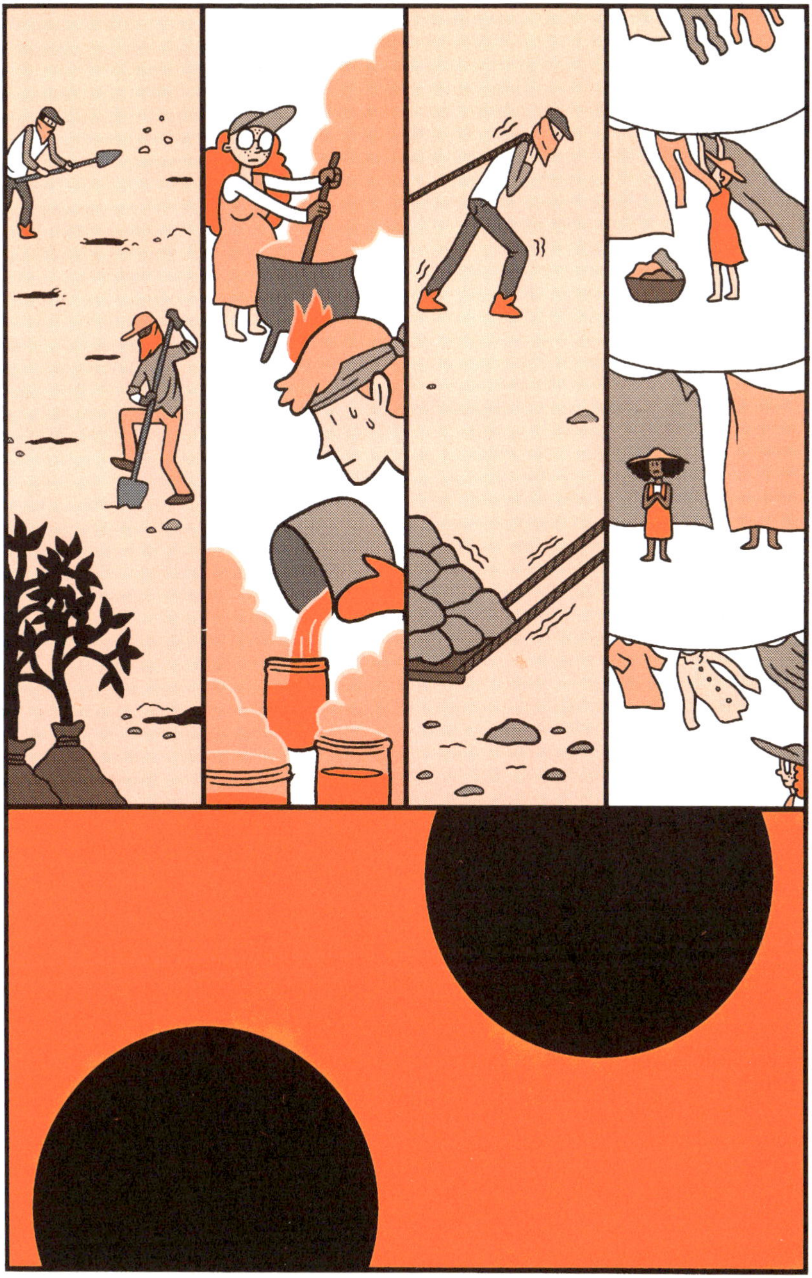

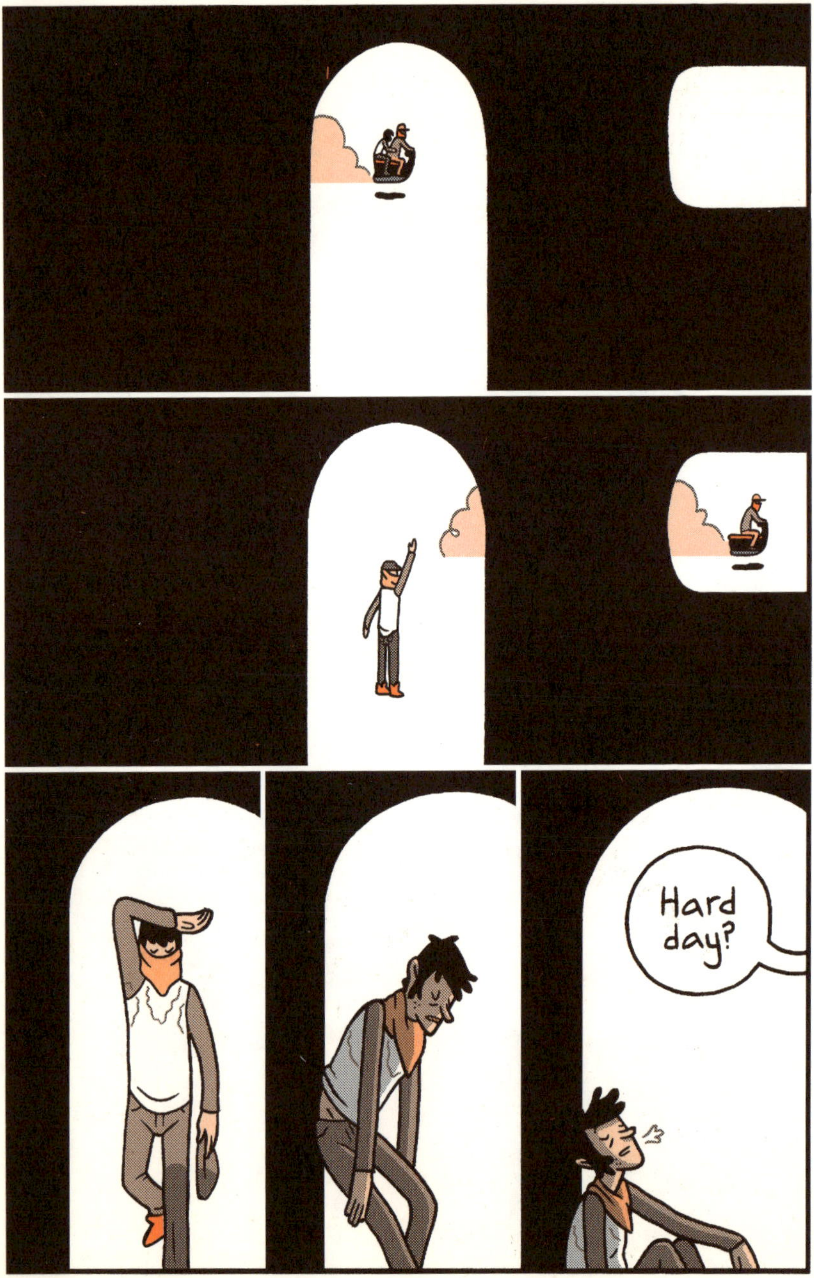
Hard day?

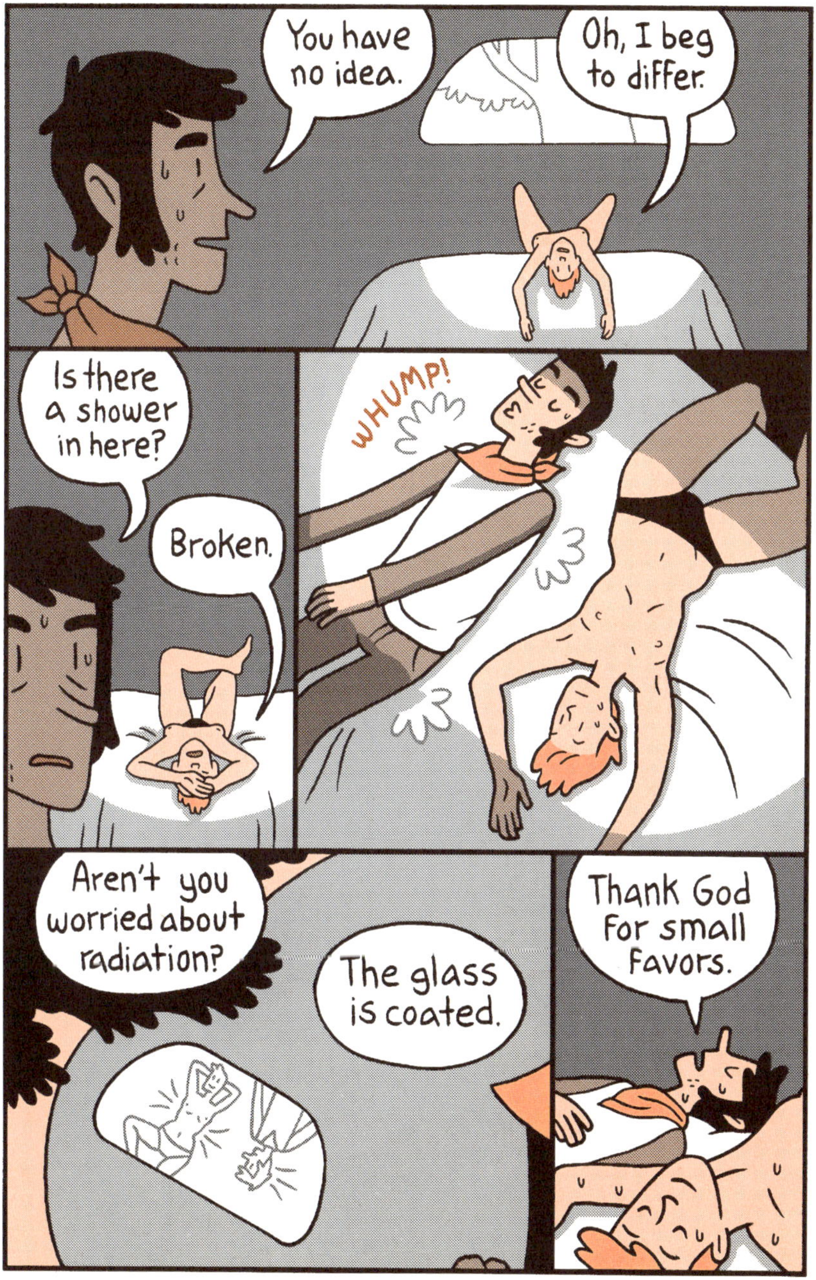
You have no idea.
Oh, I beg to differ.
Is there a shower in here?
Broken.
WHUMP!
Aren't you worried about radiation?
The glass is coated.
Thank God for small favors.

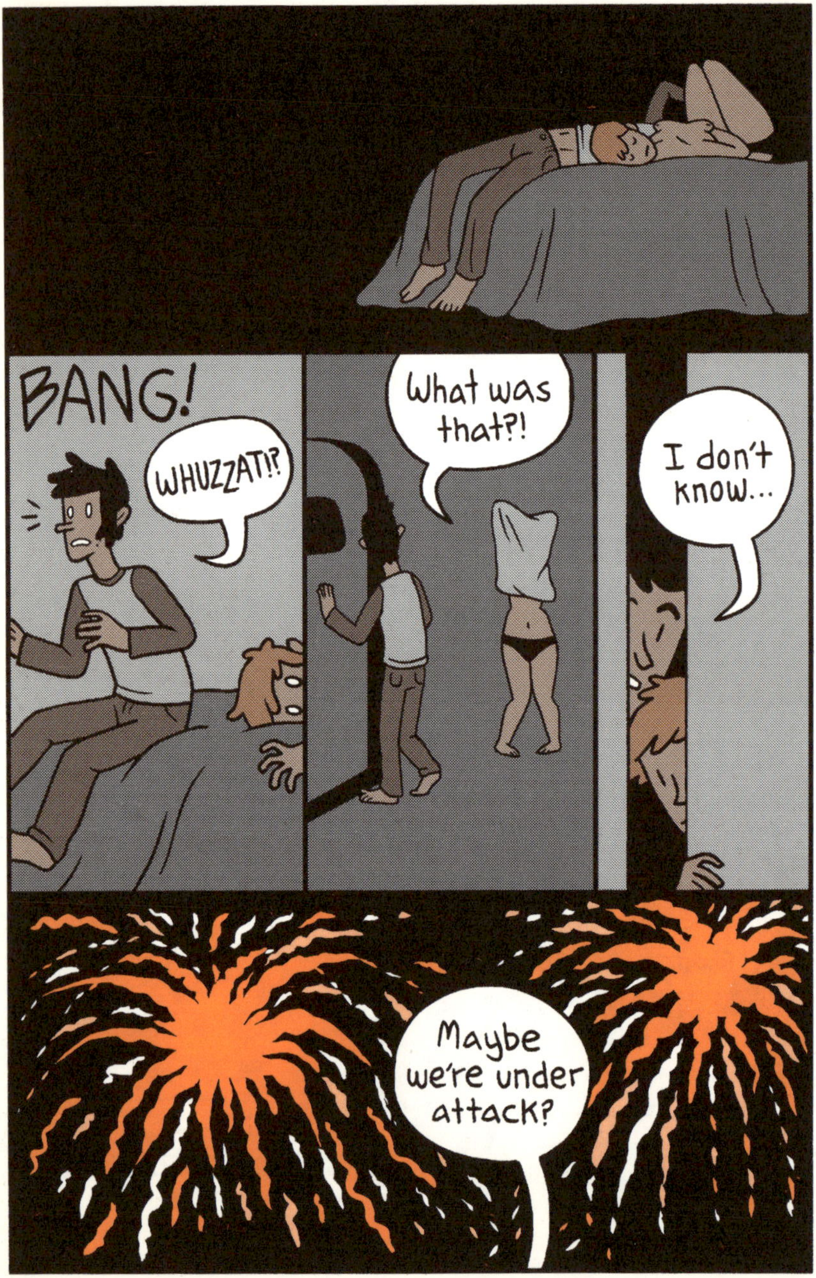
BANG!
WHUZZAT!?
What was that?!
I don't know...
Maybe we're under attack?

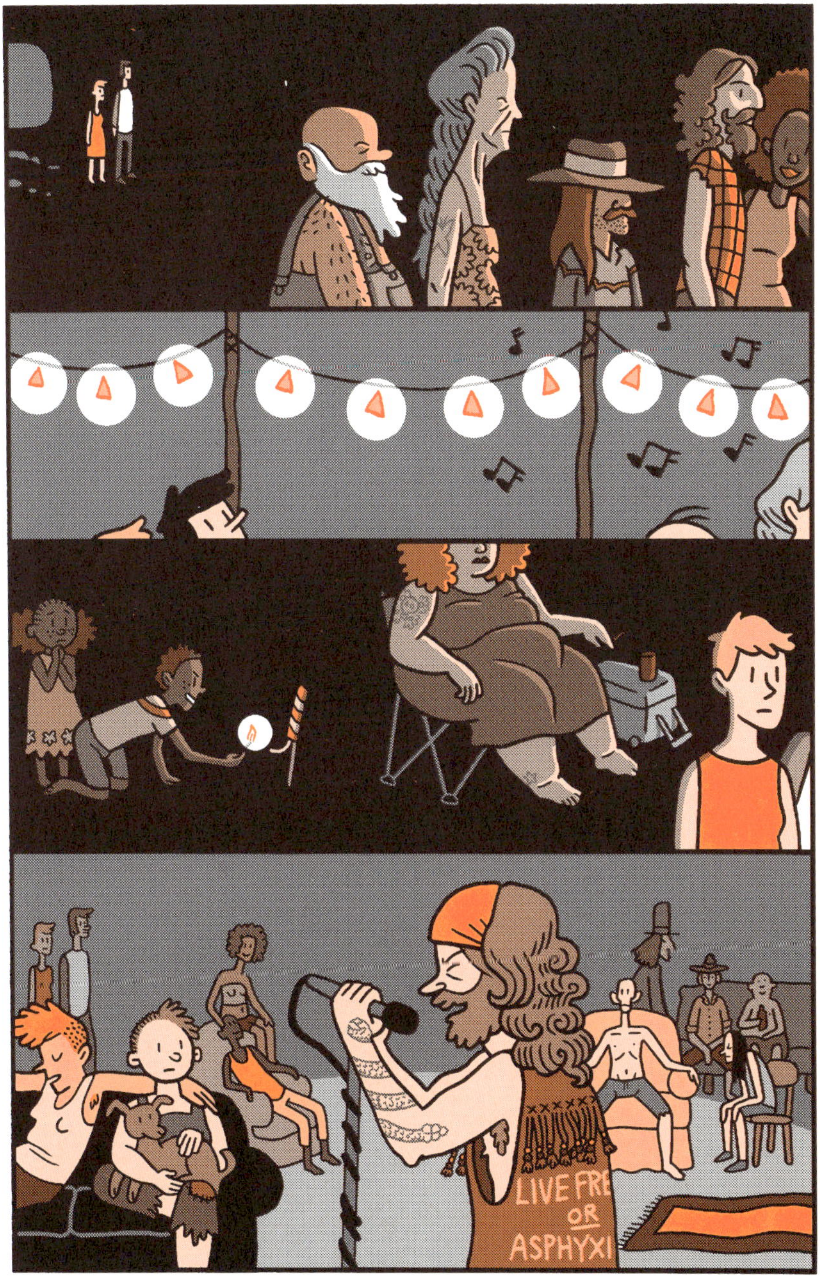
LIVE FRE
OR
ASPHYXI

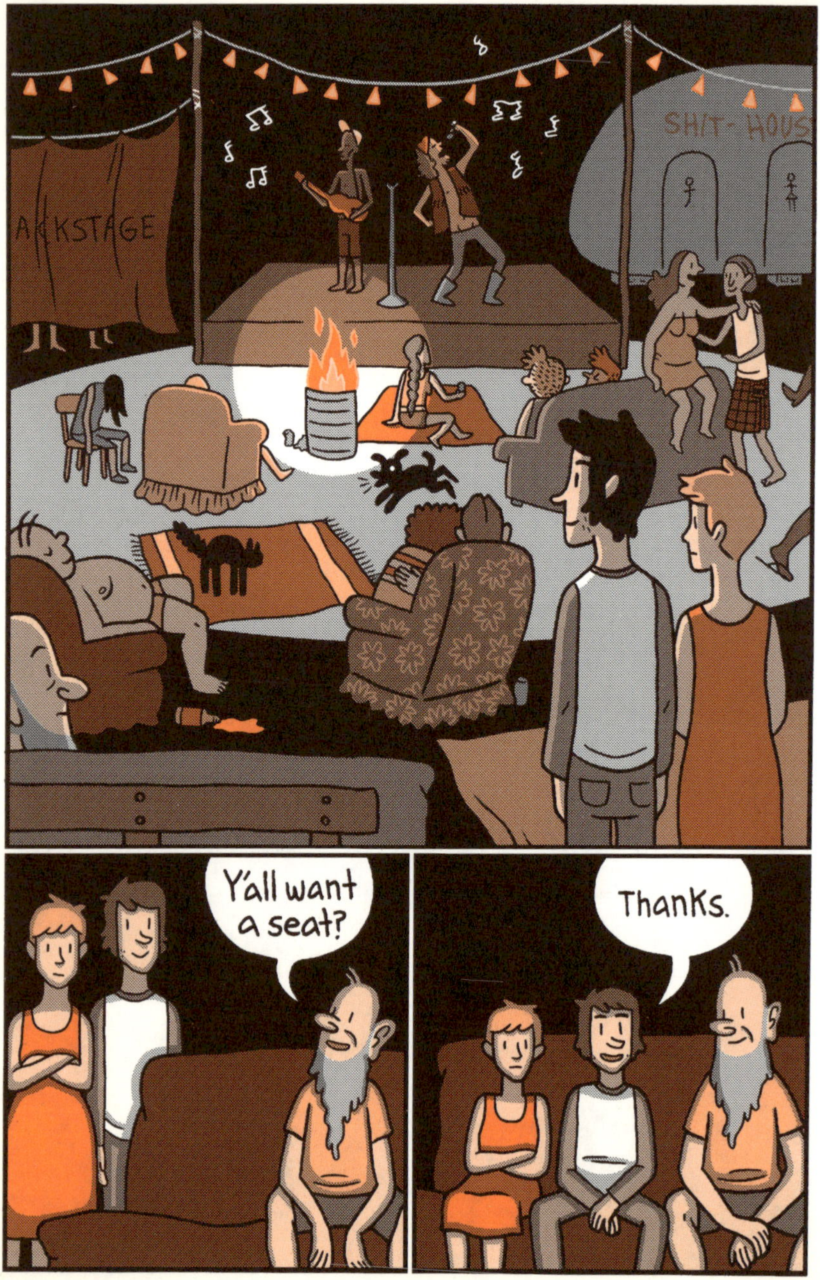

ACKSTAGE
SHIT-HOUS
Y'all want a seat?
Thanks.

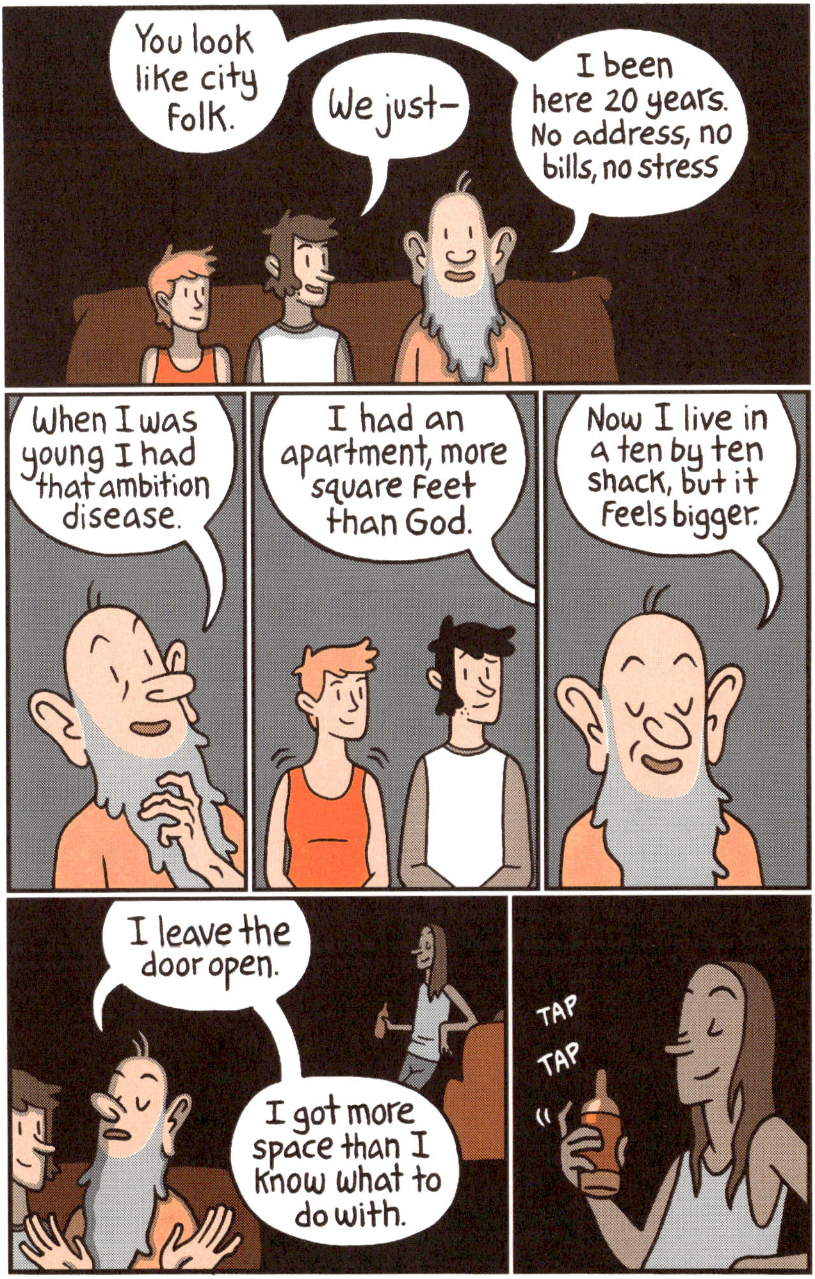
You look like city folk.
We just-
I been here 20 years. No address, no bills, no stress
When I was young I had that ambition disease.
I had an apartment, more square feet than God.
Now I live in a ten by ten shack, but it feels bigger.
I leave the door open.
I got more space than I know what to do with.
TAP
TAP

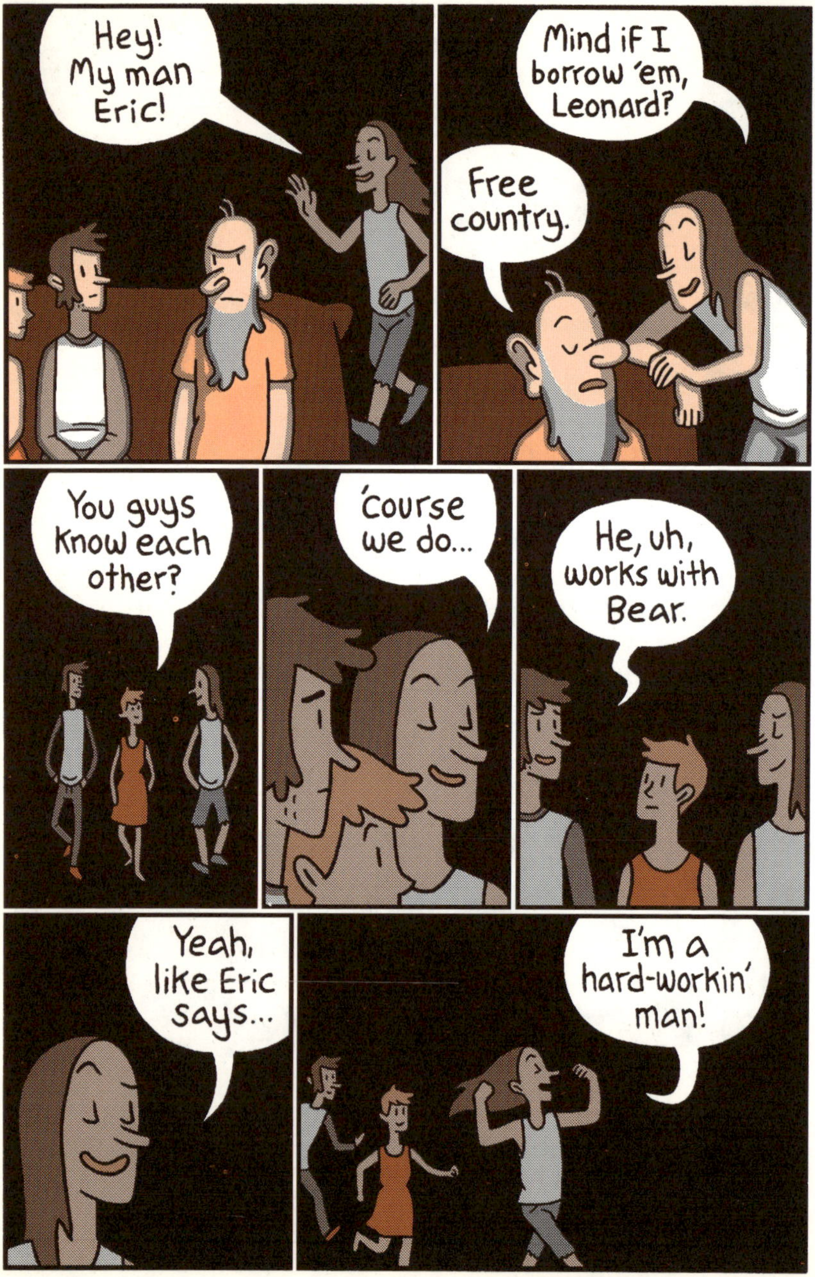
Hey! My man Eric!
Mind if I borrow 'em, Leonard?
Free country.
You guys know each other?
'Course we do...
He, uh, works with Bear.
Yeah, like Eric says...
I'm a hard-workin' man!

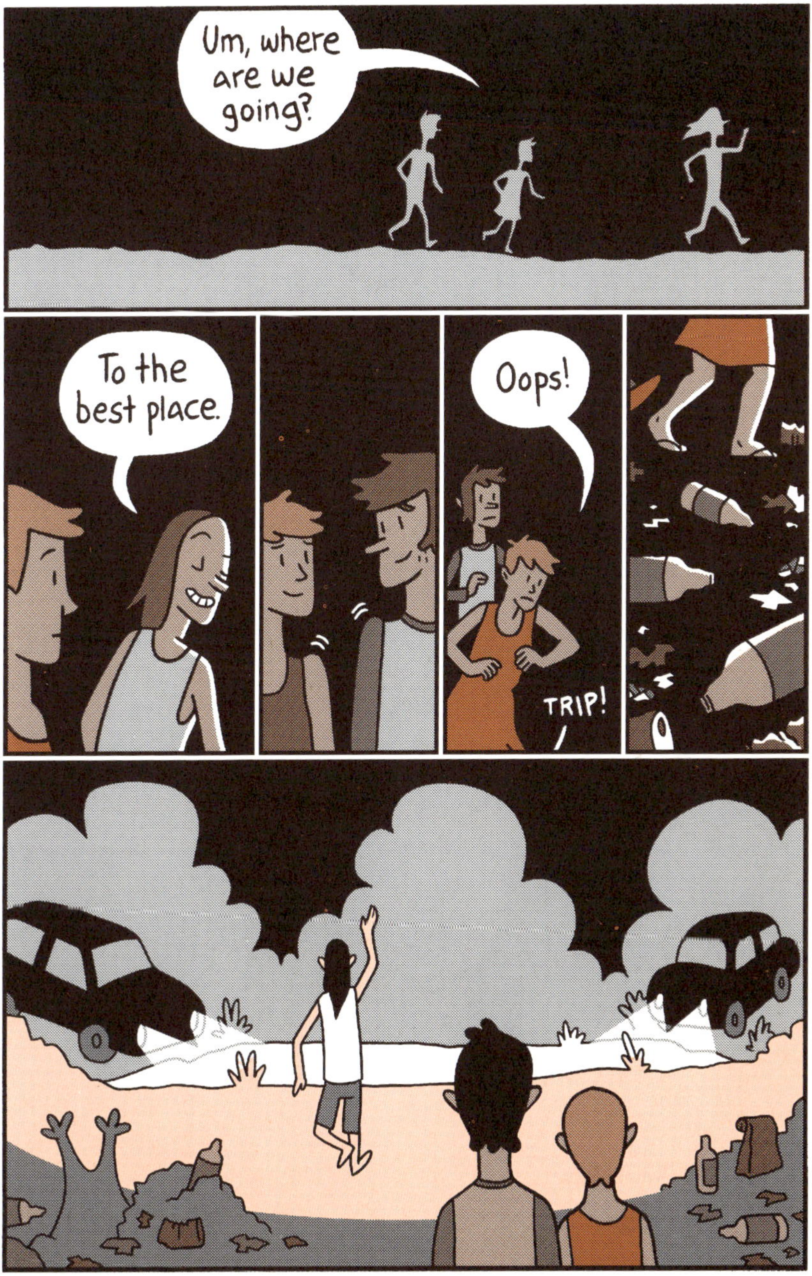
Um, where are we going?
To the best place.
Oops!
TRIP!

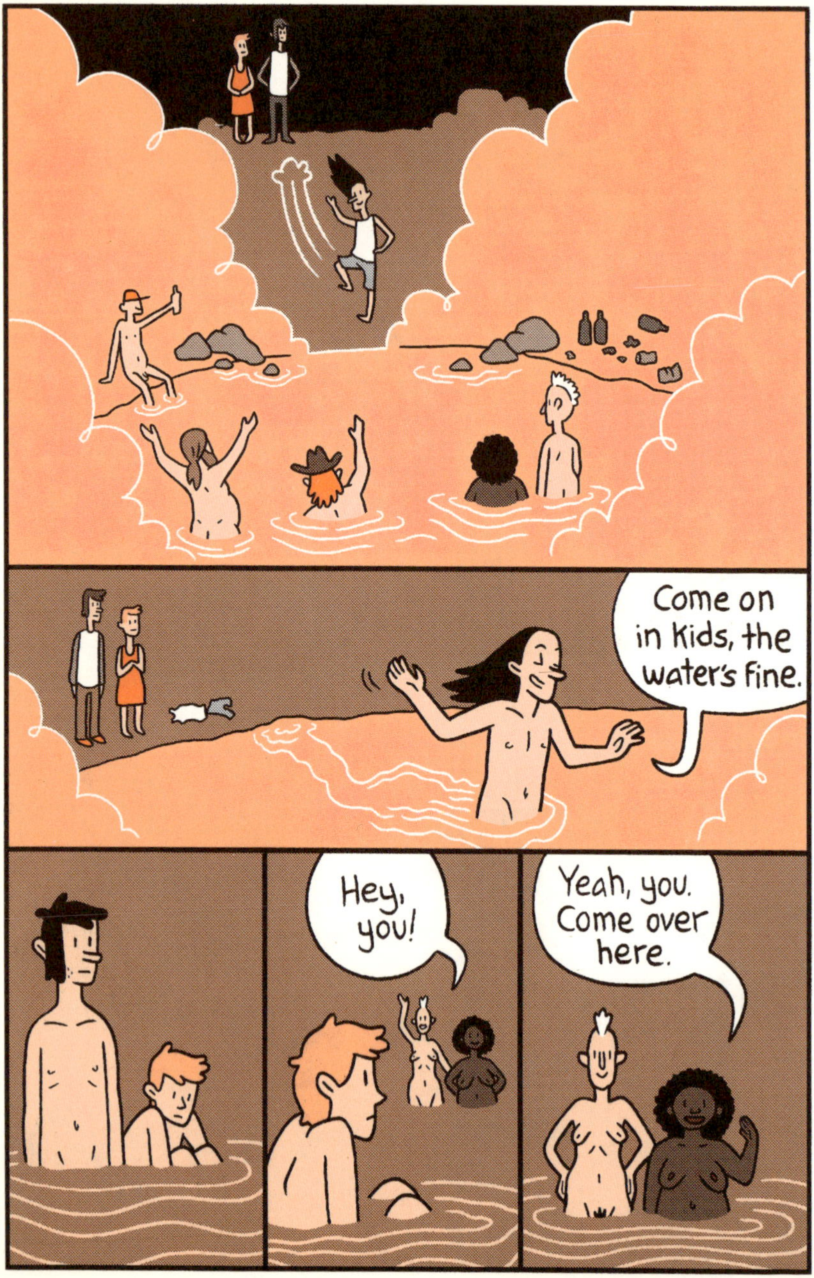
Come on in Kids, the water's fine.
Hey, you!
Yeah, you. Come over here.

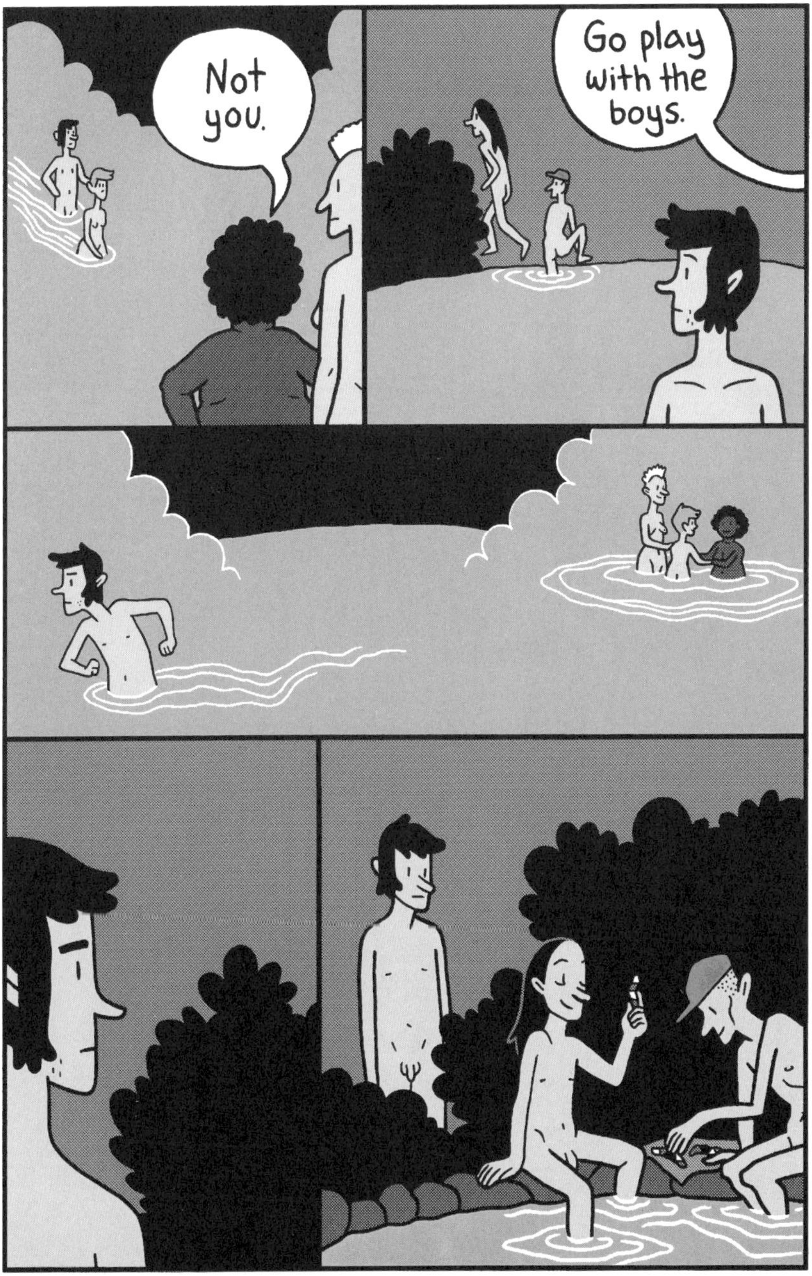
Not you.
Go play with the boys.

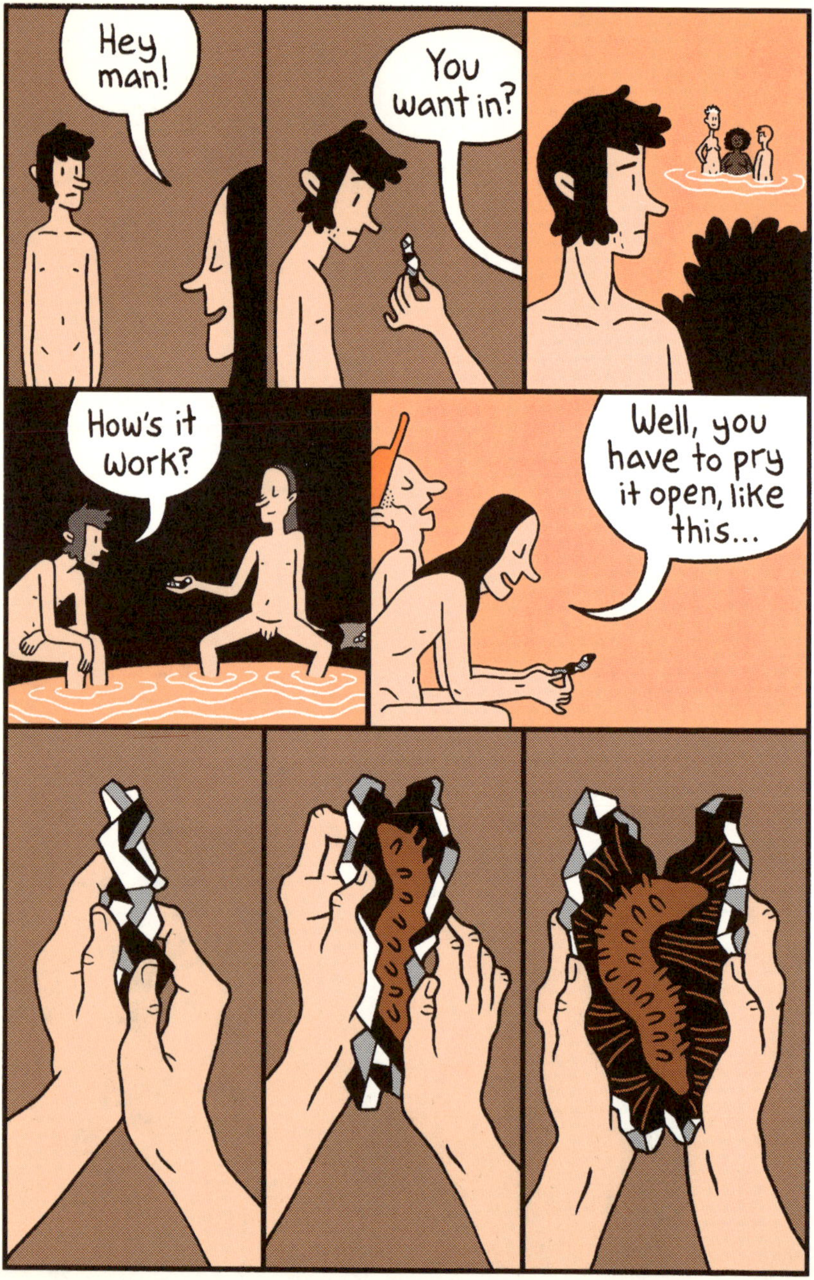
Hey man!
You want in?
How's it work?
Well, you have to pry it open, like this...

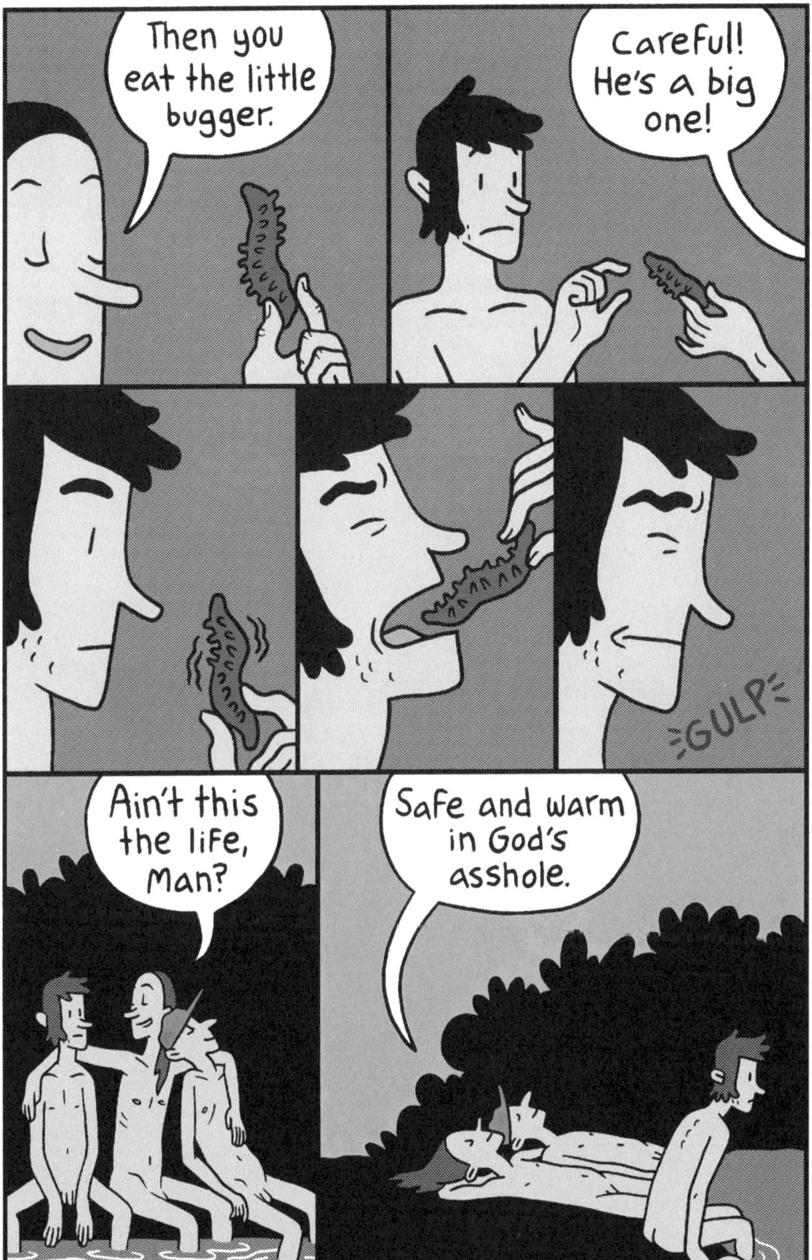
Then you eat the little bugger.
Careful! He's a big one!
GULP
Ain't this the life, Man?
Safe and warm in God's asshole.

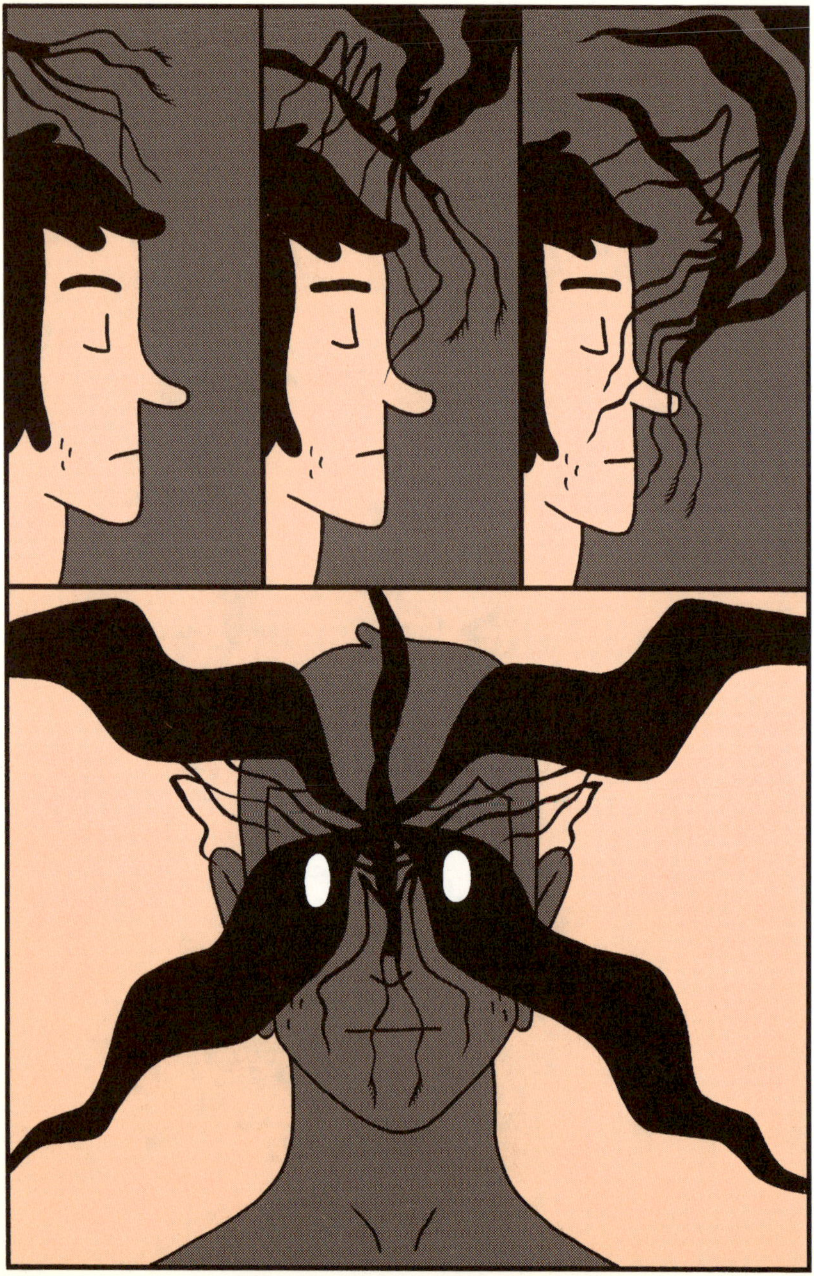

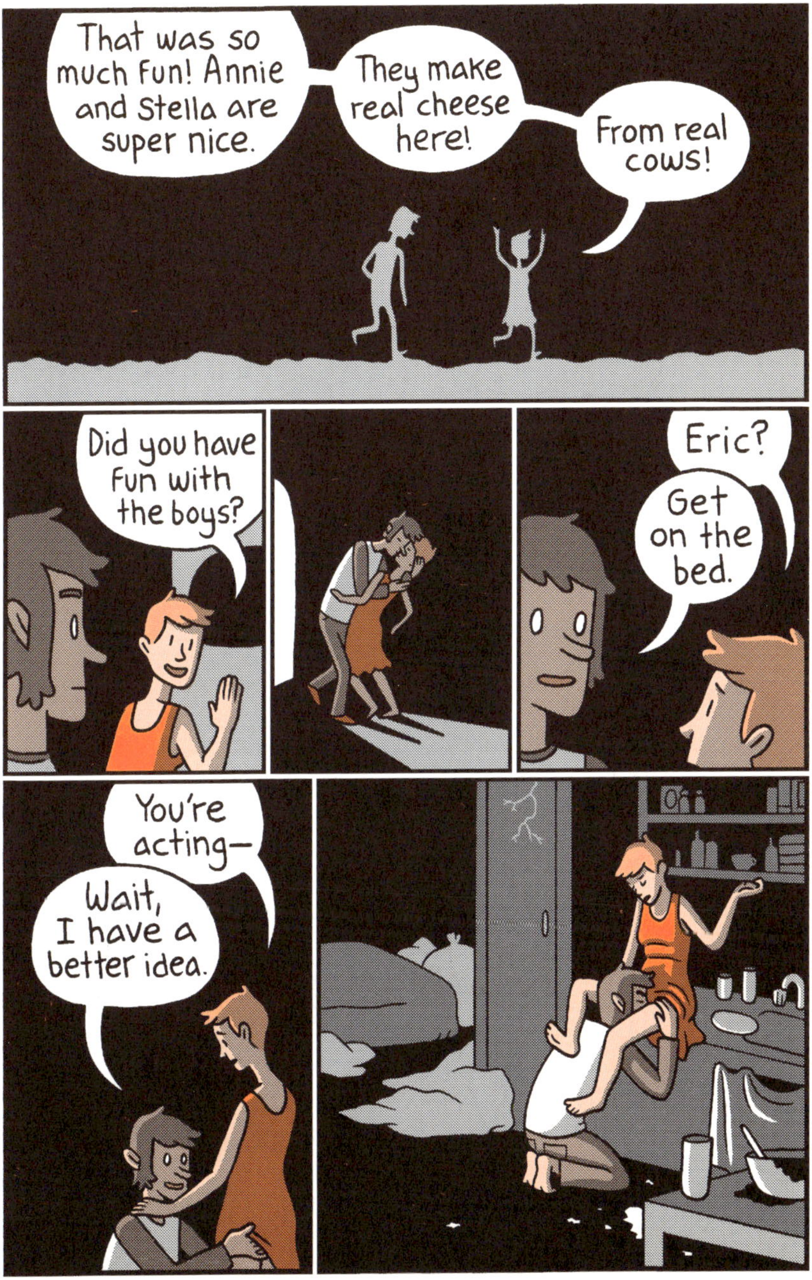
That was so much fun! Annie and Stella are super nice.
They make real cheese here!
From real cows!
Did you have fun with the boys?
Eric?
Get on the bed.
You're acting—
Wait, I have a better idea.

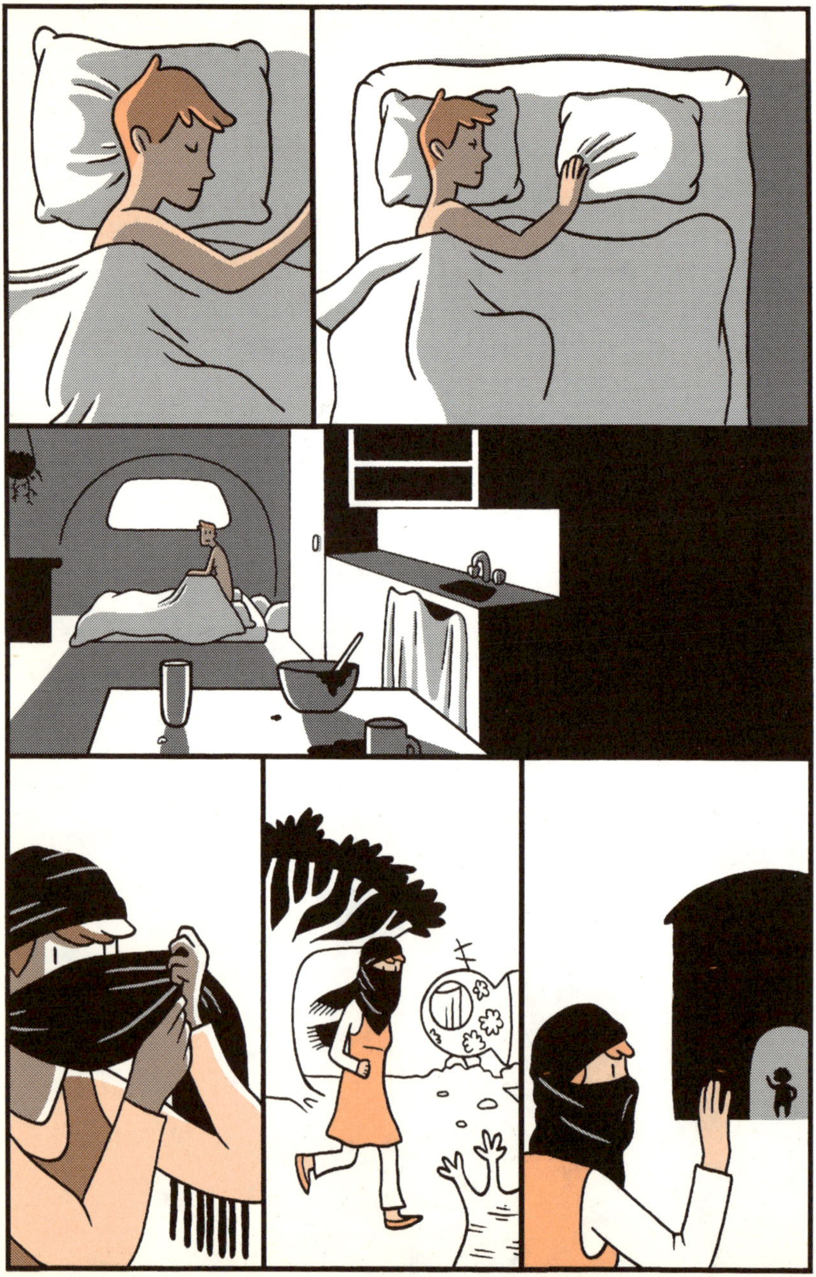

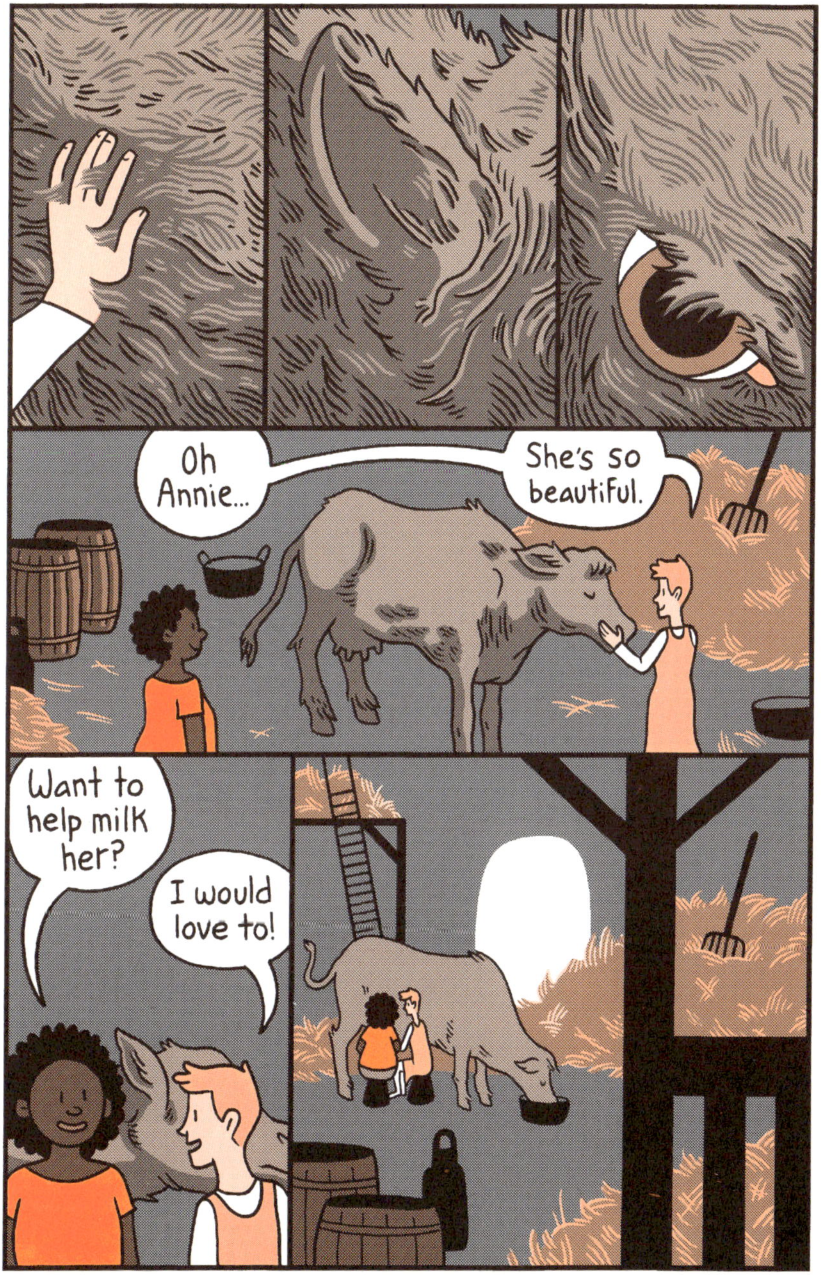
Oh Annie...
She's so beautiful.
Want to help milk her?
I would love to!

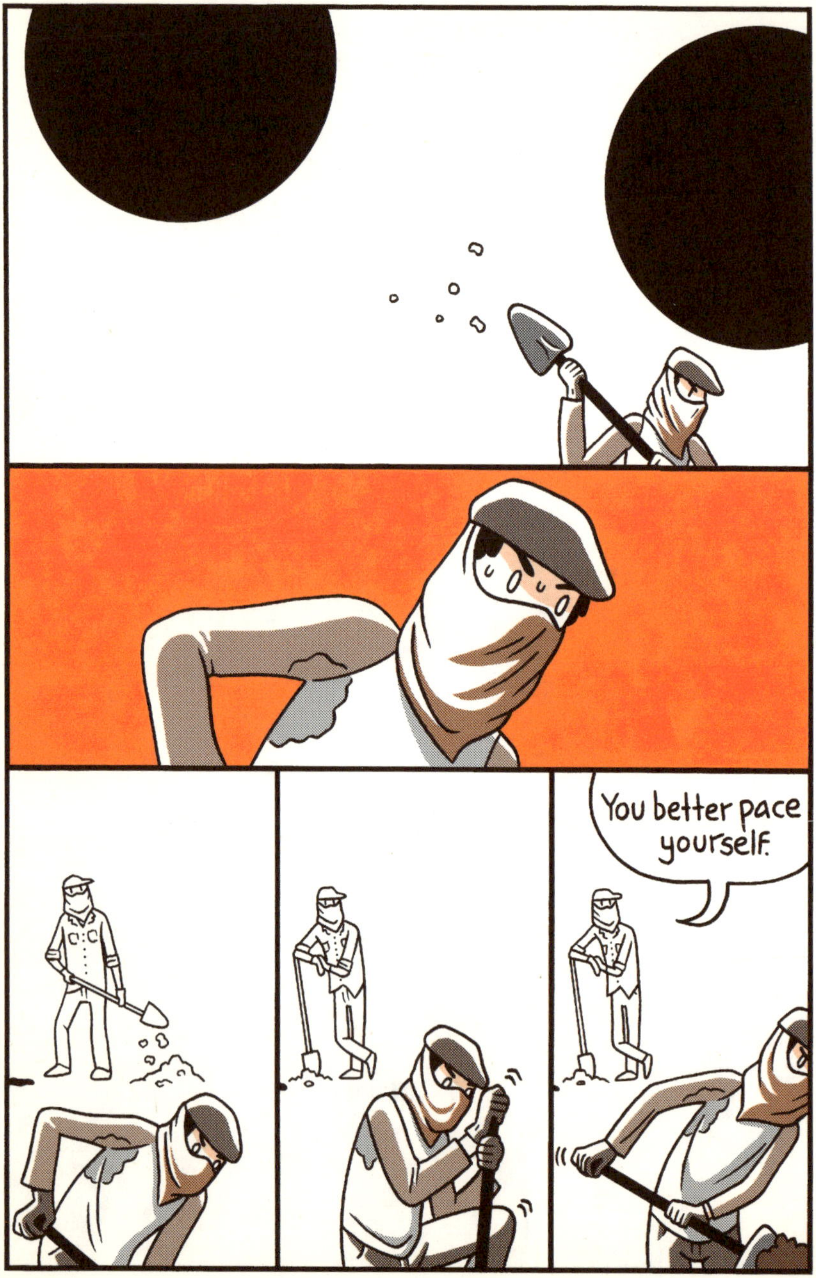
You better pace yourself.

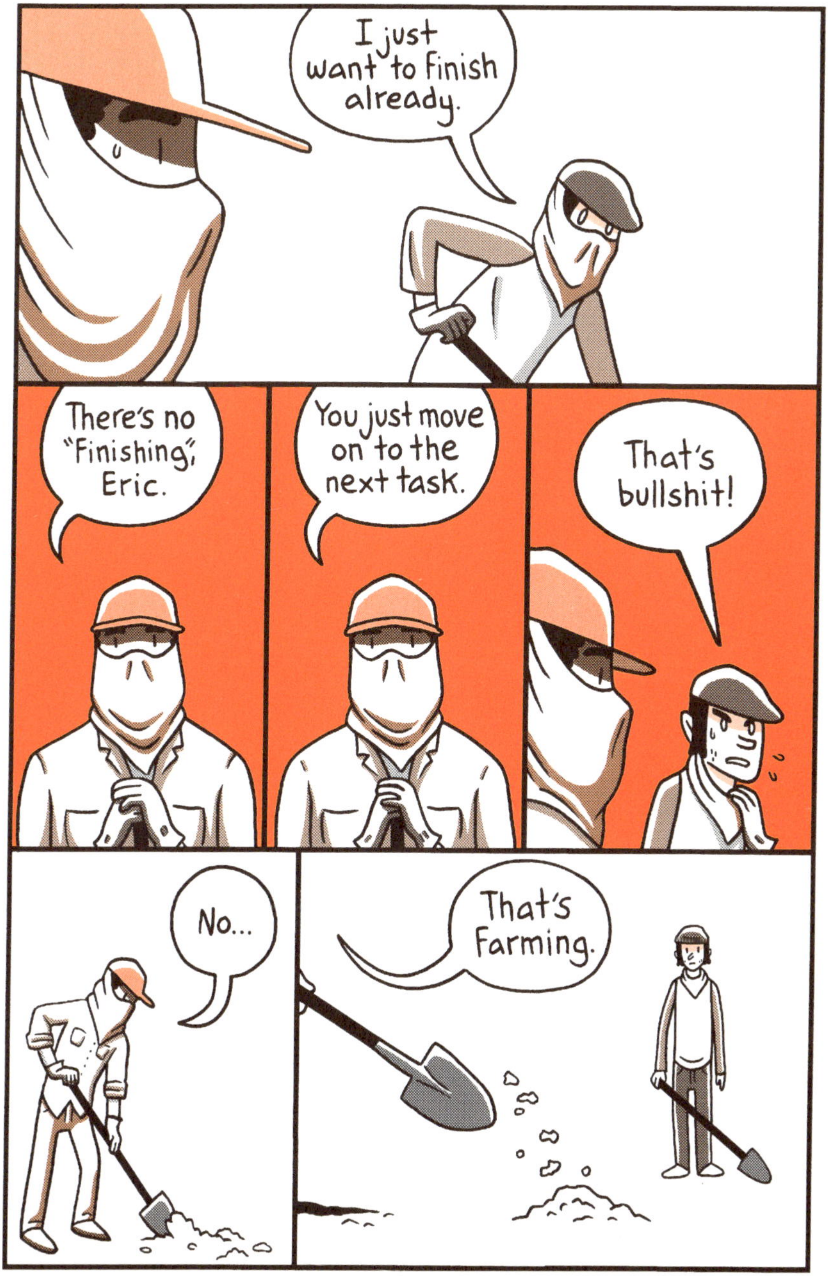
I just want to finish already.
There's no "Finishing," Eric.
You just move on to the next task.
That's bullshit!
No...
That's Farming.

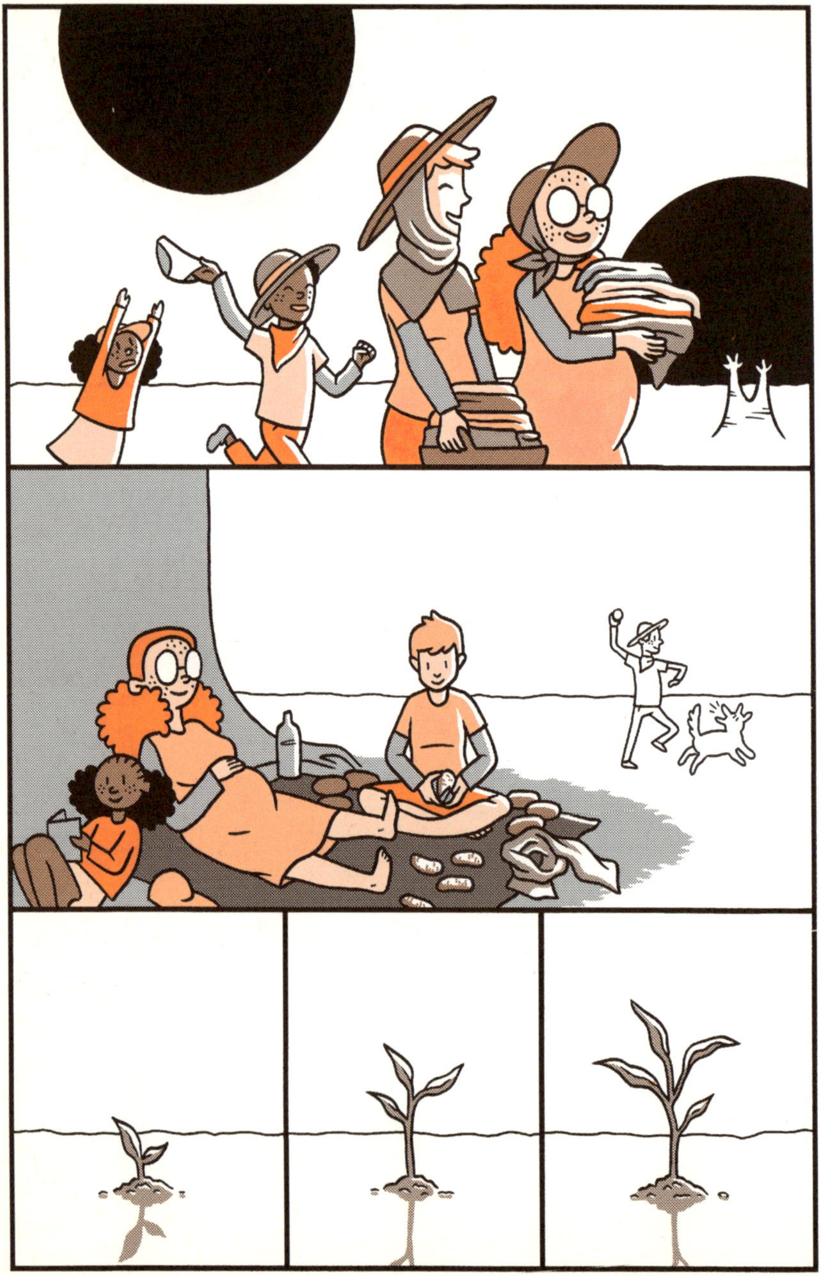

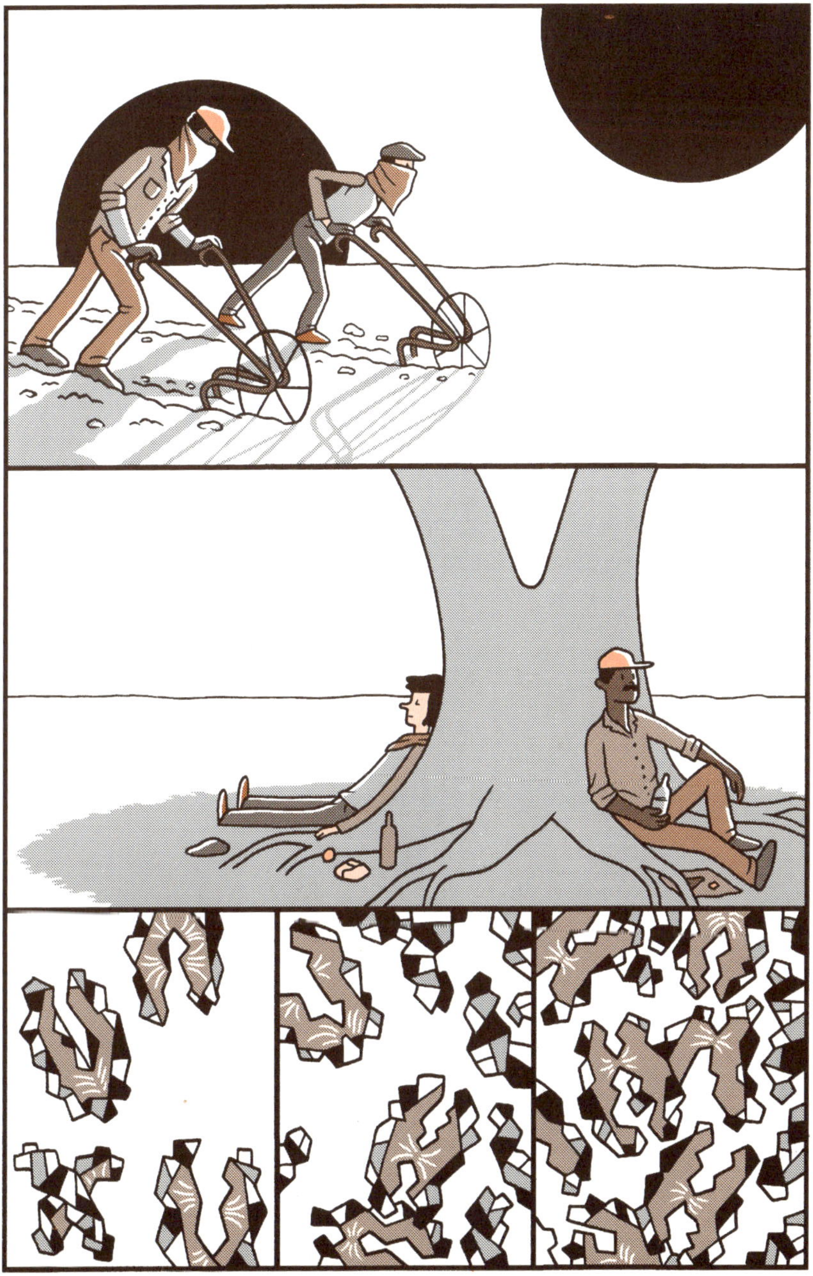

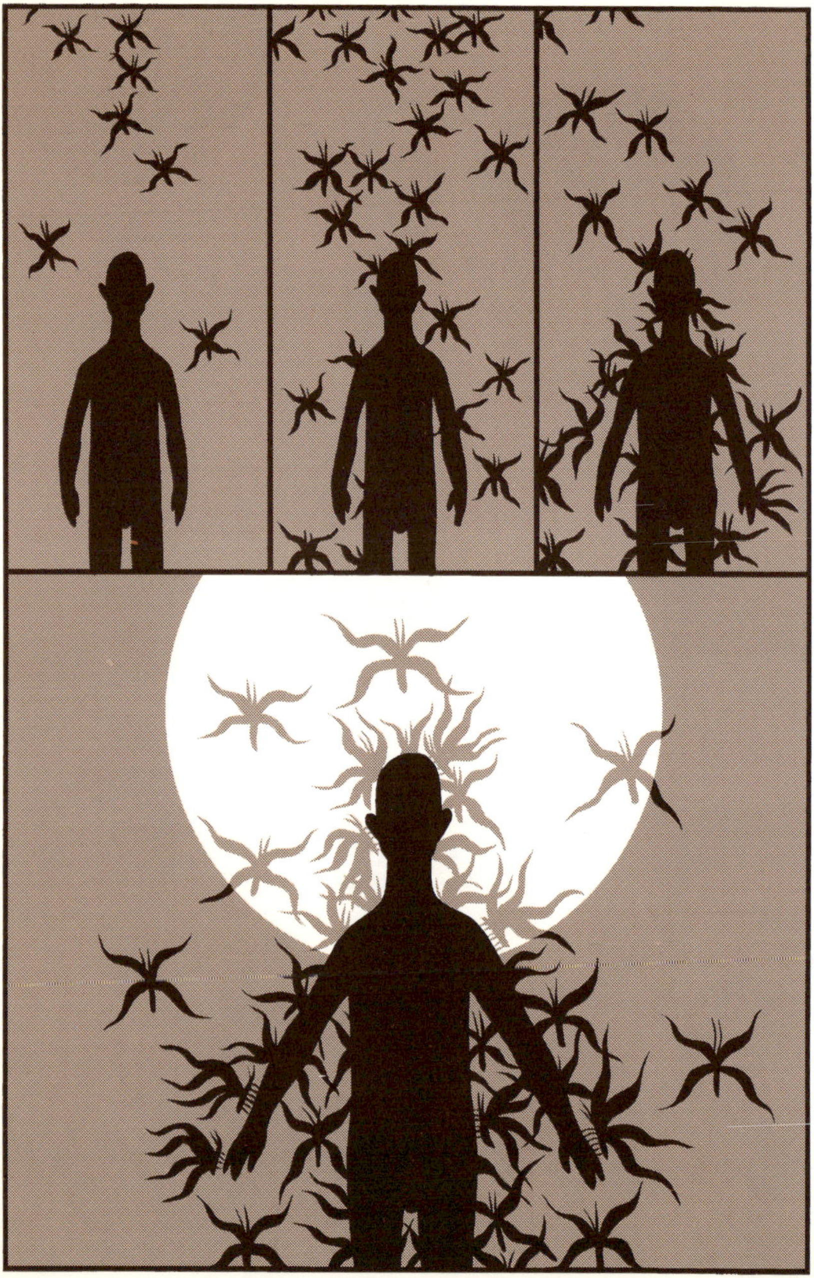

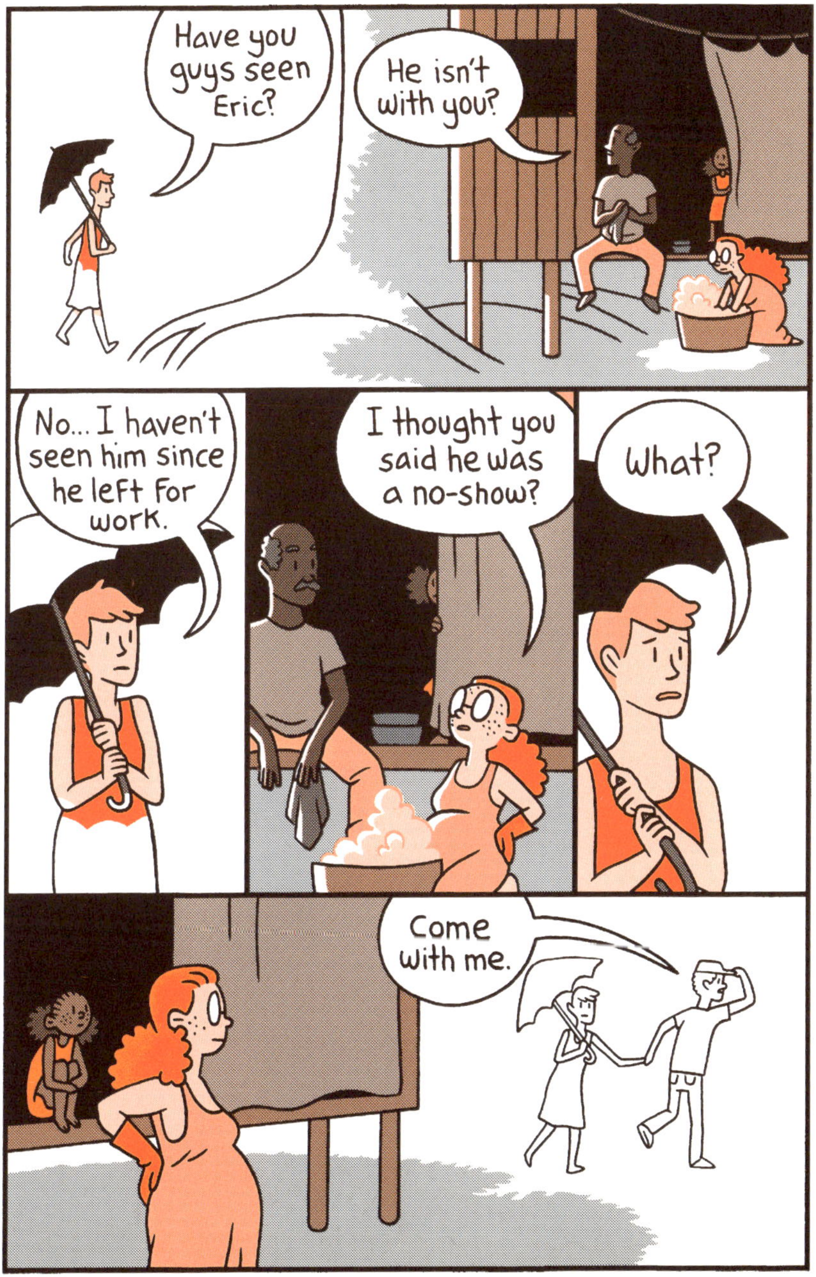
Have you guys seen Eric?
He isn't with you?
No... I haven't seen him since he left for work.
I thought you said he was a no-show?
What?
Come with me.

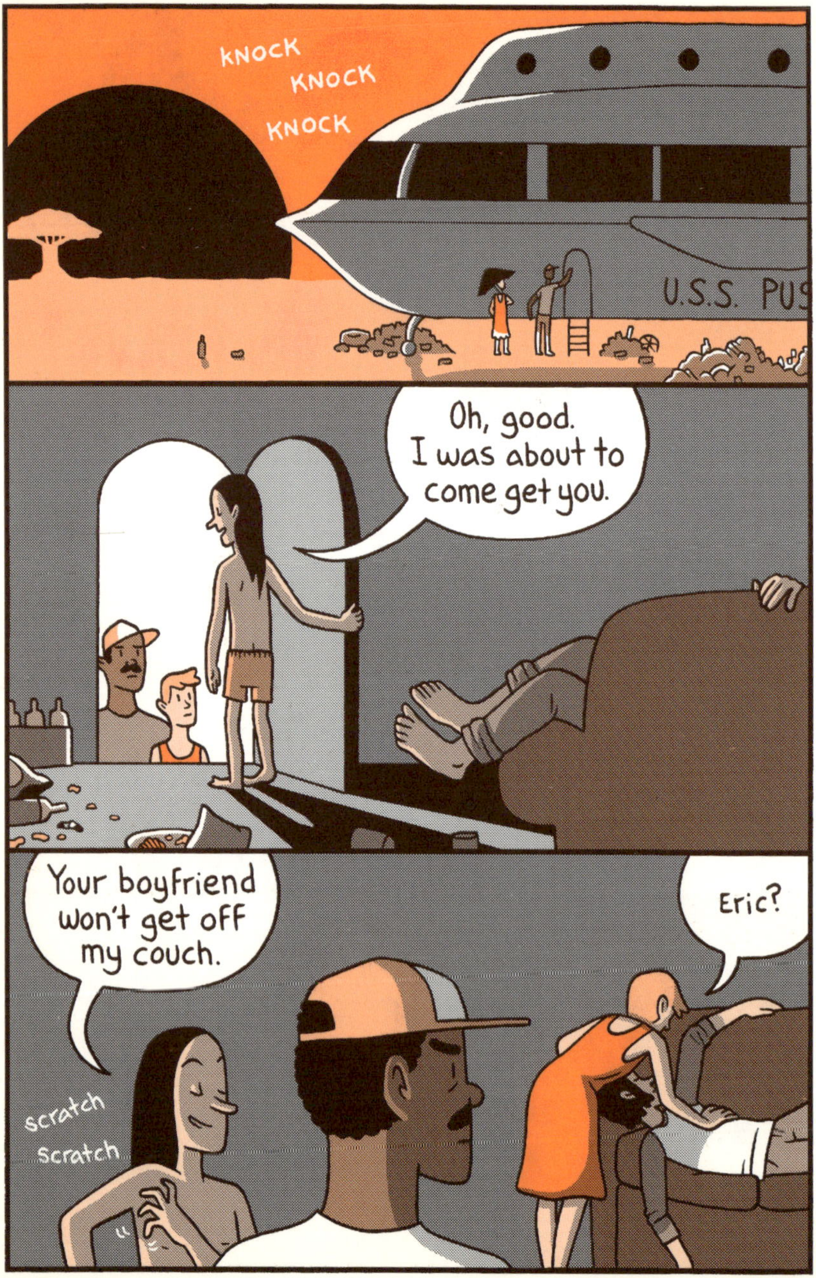
KNOCK
KNOCK
KNOCK
U.S.S. PUS
Oh, good. I was about to come get you.
Your boyfriend won't get off my couch.
Eric?
scratch
scratch

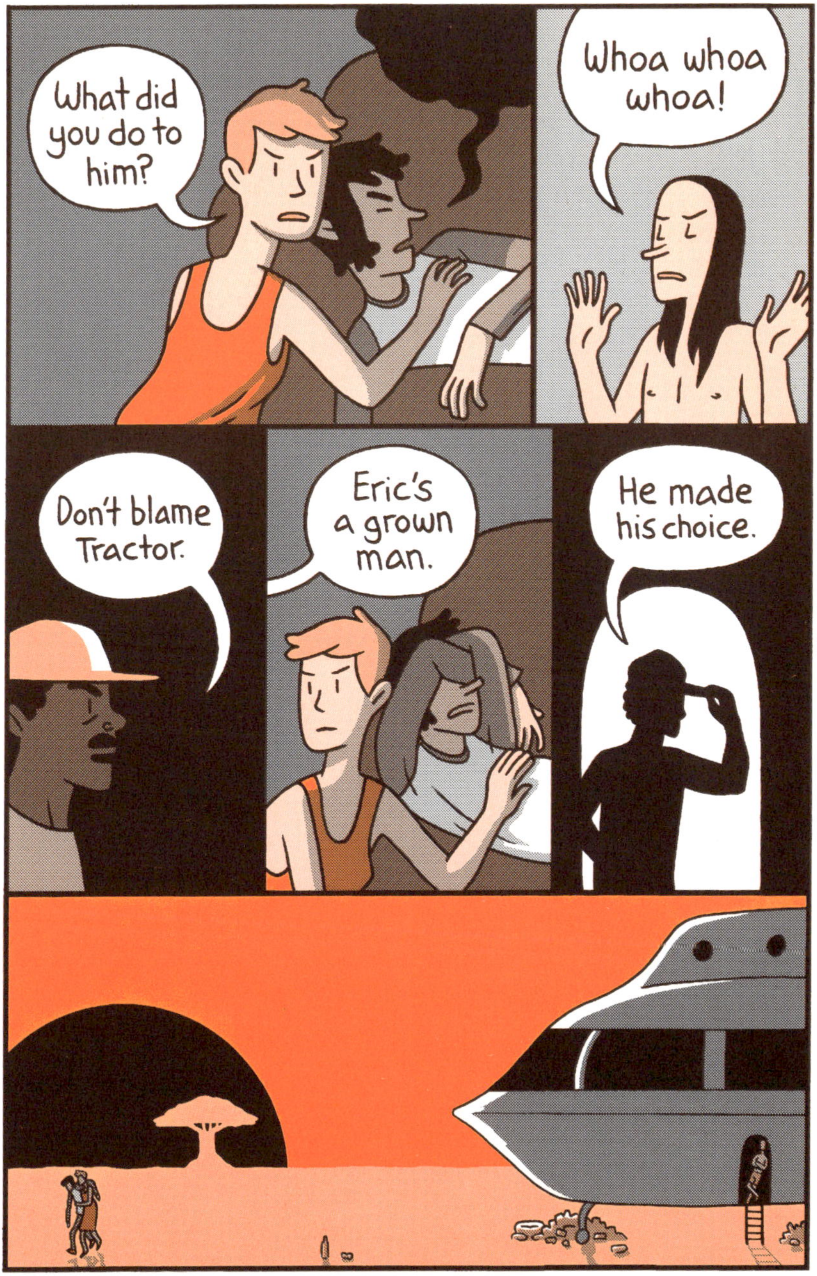
What did you do to him?
Whoa whoa whoa!
Don't blame Tractor.
Eric's a grown man.
He made his choice.

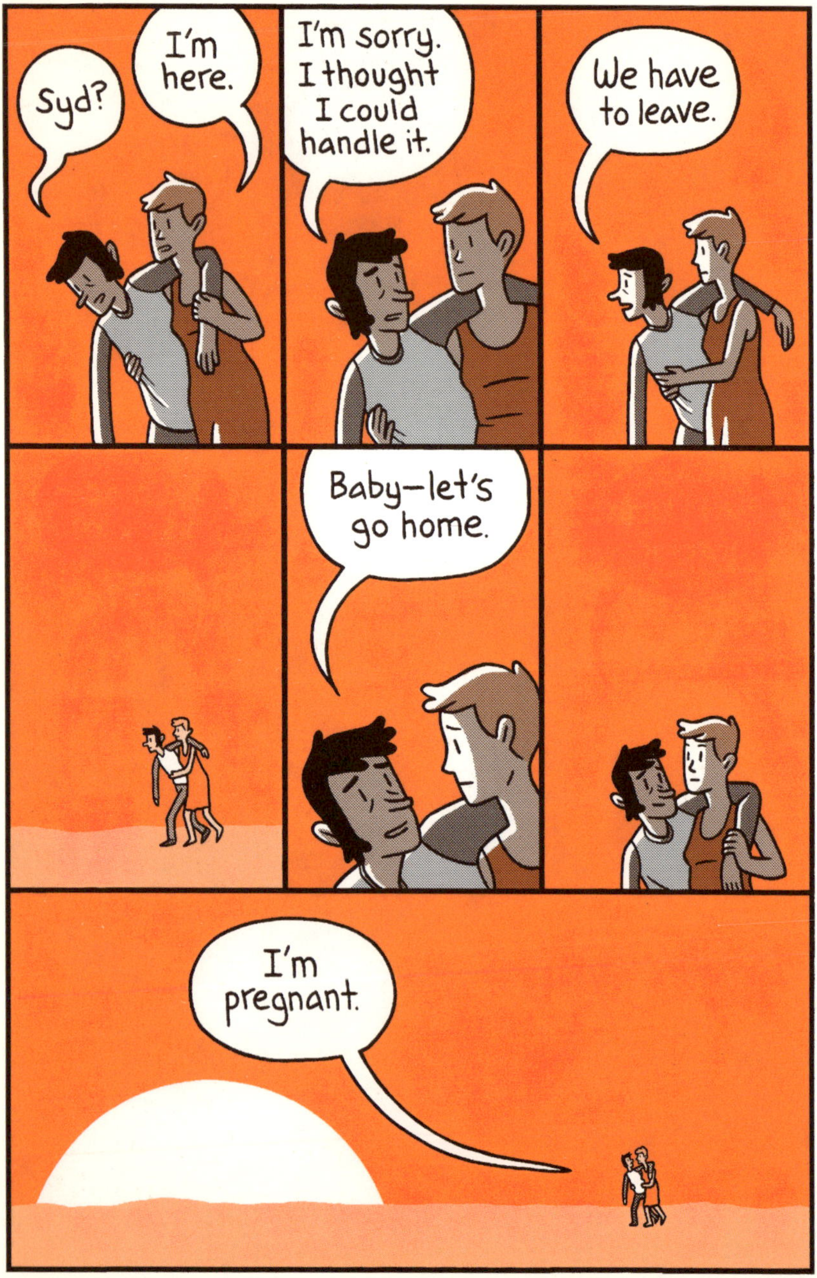
Syd?
I'm here.
I'm sorry. I thought I could handle it.
We have to leave.
Baby—let's go home.
I'm pregnant.

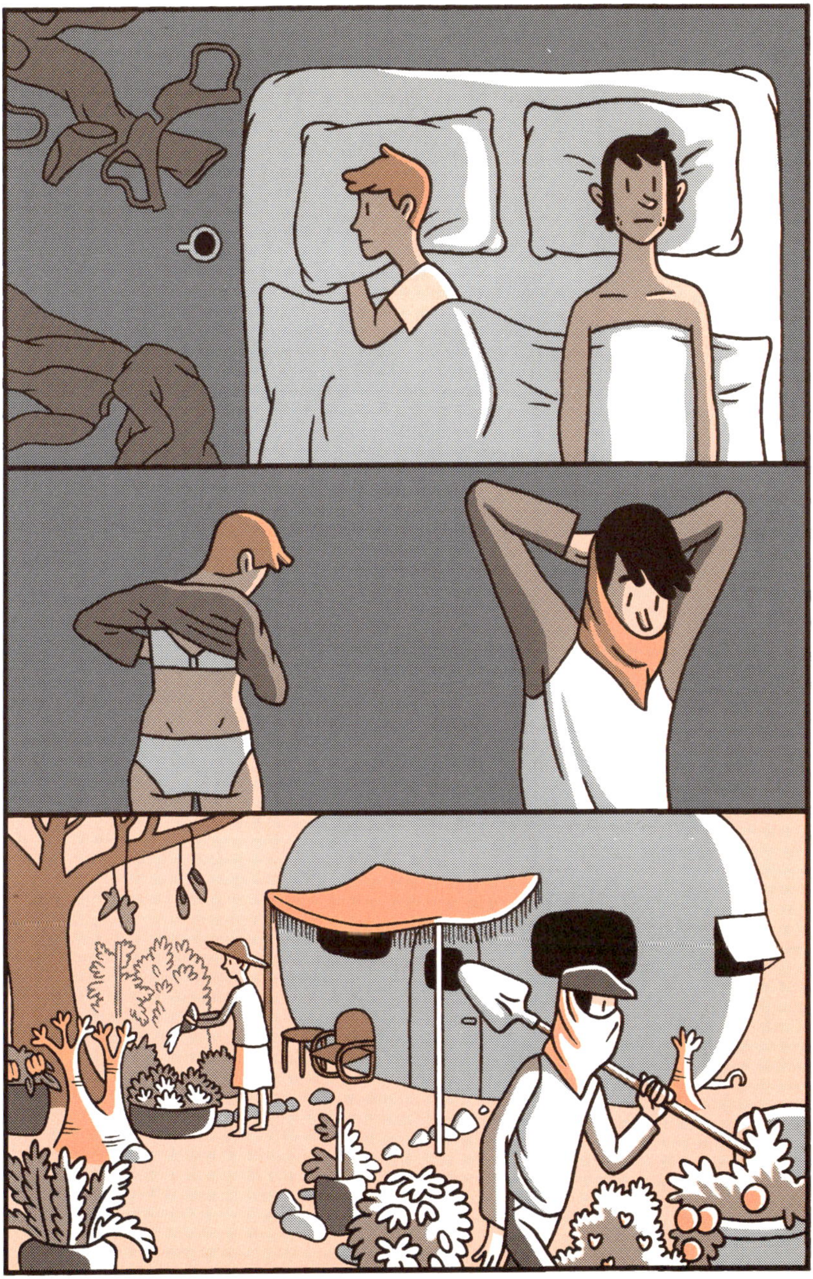

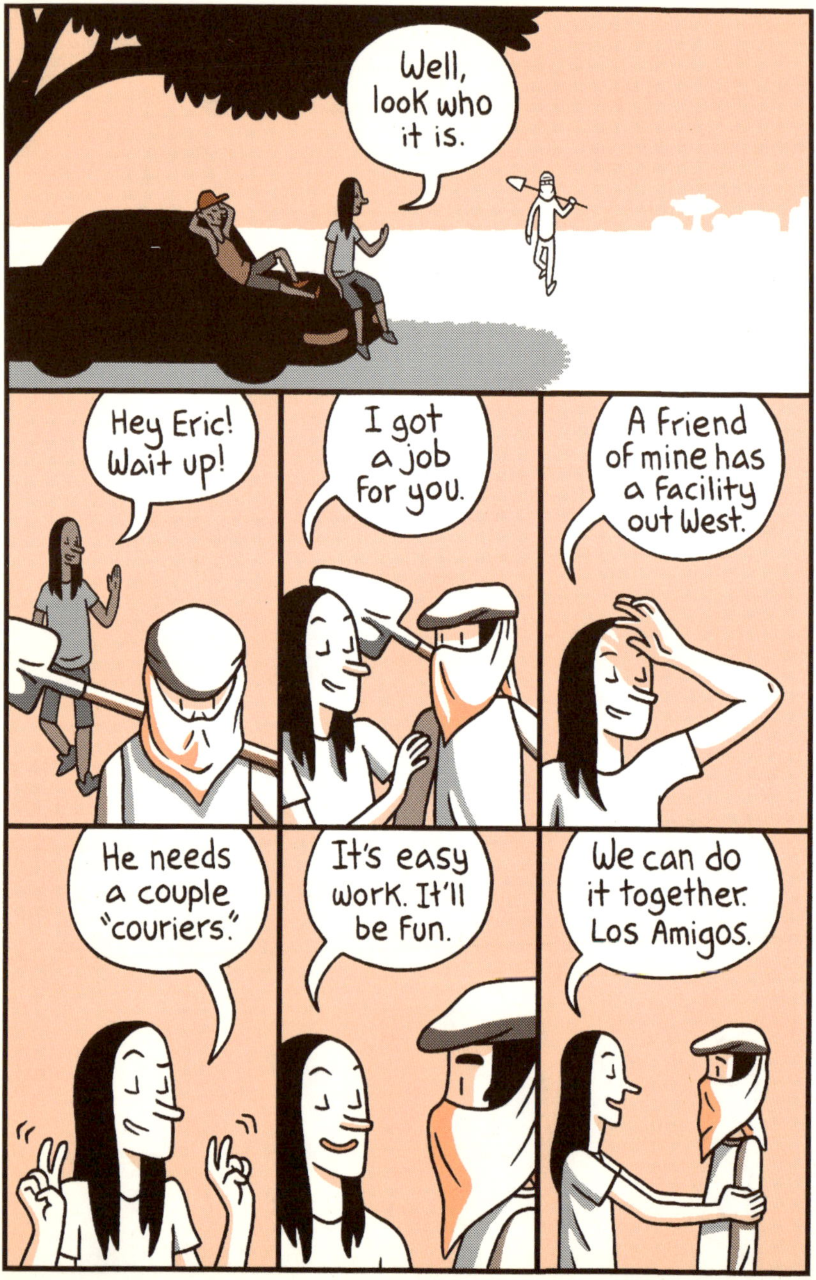
Well, look who it is.
Hey Eric! Wait up!
I got a job for you.
A friend of mine has a facility out West.
He needs a couple "couriers."
It's easy work. It'll be fun.
We can do it together. Los Amigos.

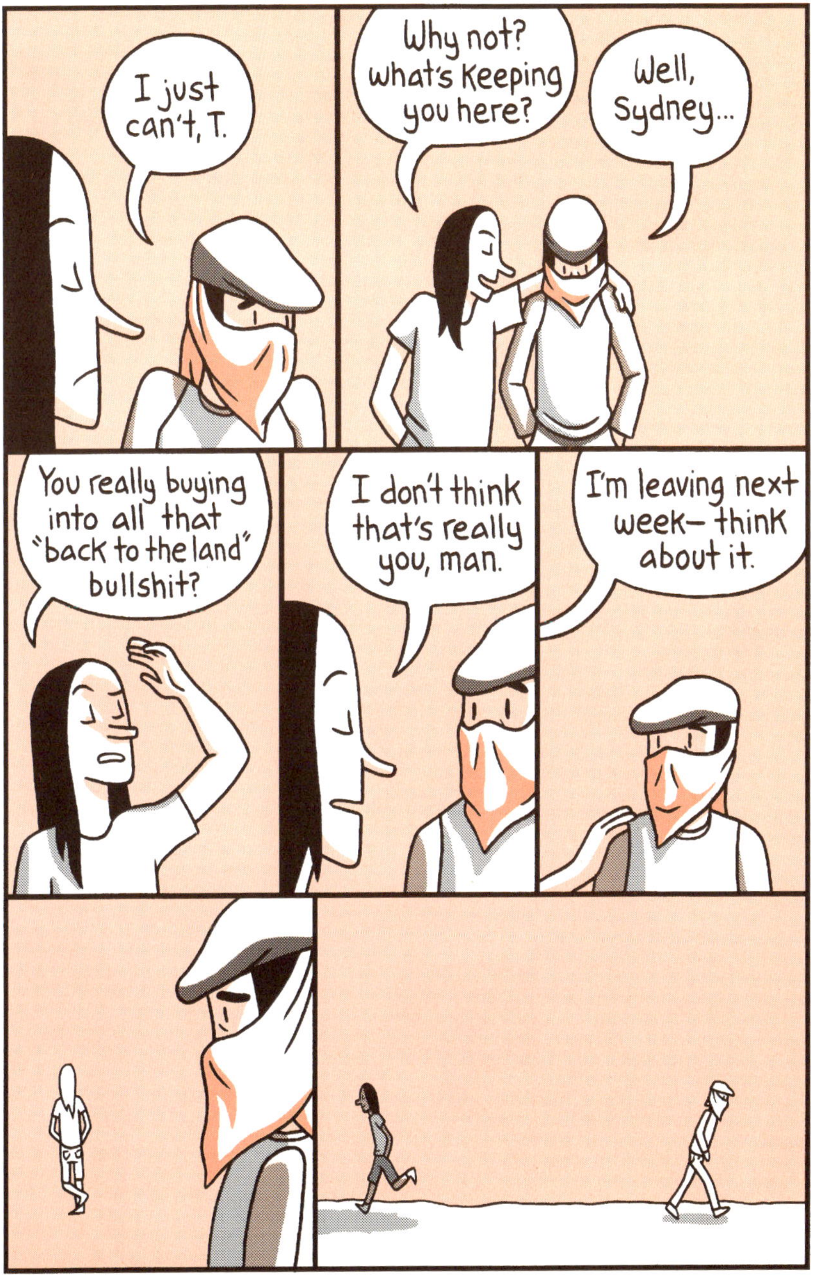
I just can't, T.
Why not? what's keeping you here?
Well, Sydney...
You really buying into all that "back to the land" bullshit?
I don't think that's really you, man.
I'm leaving next week— think about it.

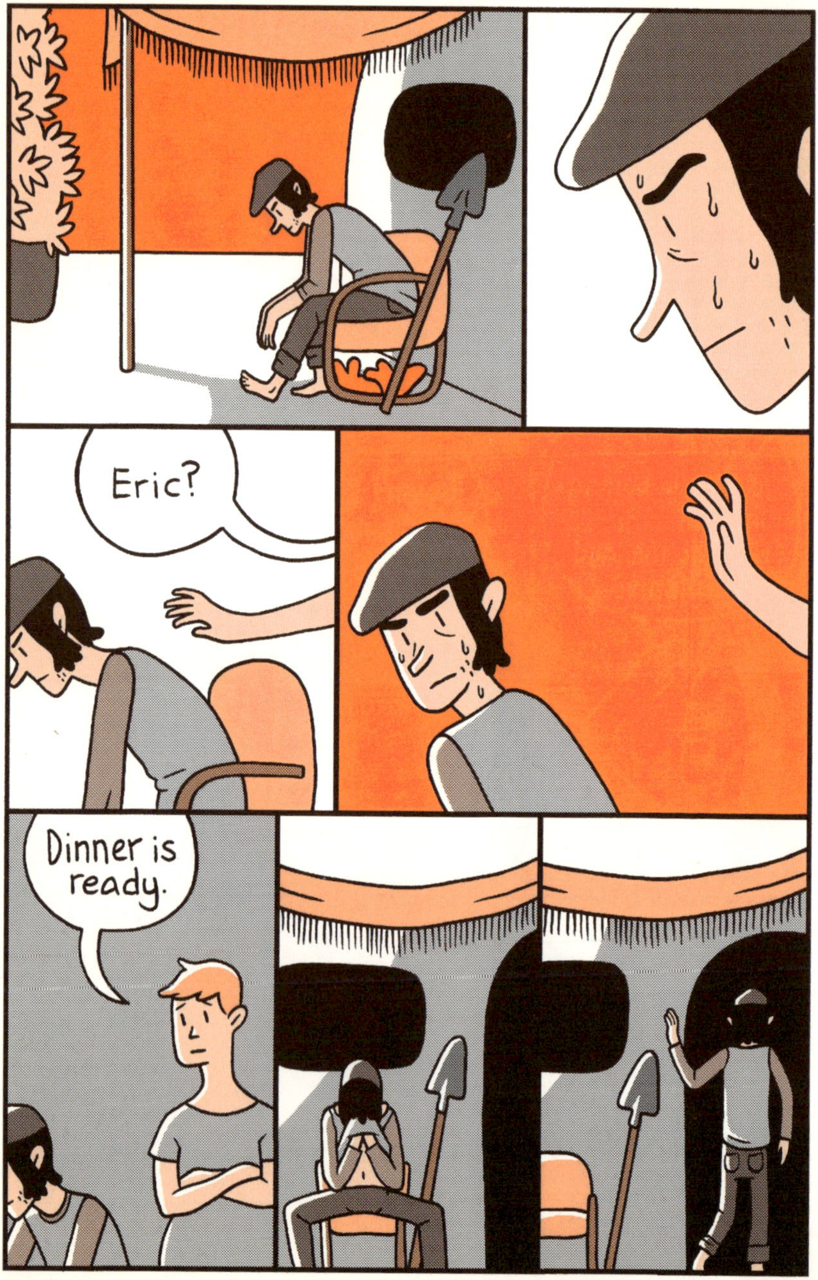
Eric?
Dinner is ready.

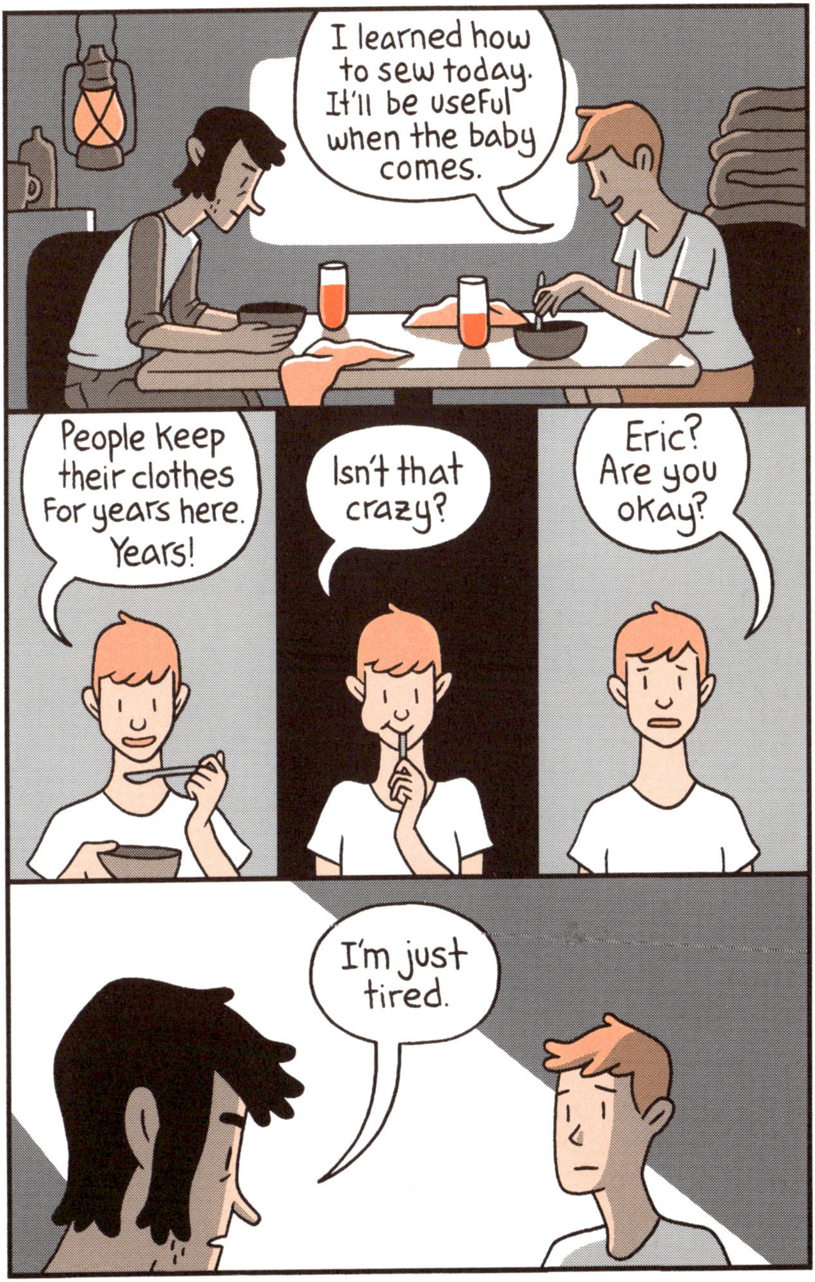
I learned how to sew today. It'll be useful when the baby comes.
People keep their clothes for years here. Years!
Isn't that crazy?
Eric? Are you okay?
I'm just tired.

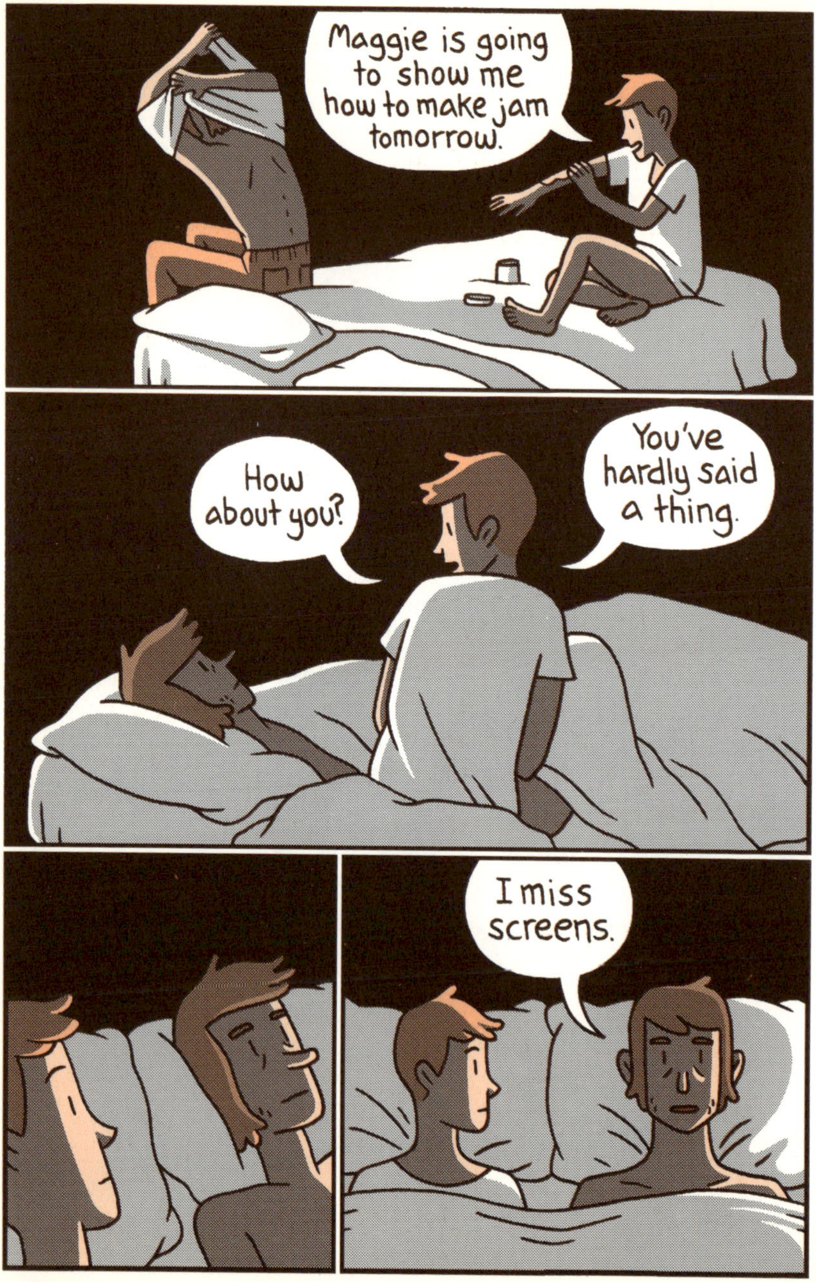
Maggie is going to show me how to make jam tomorrow.
How about you?
You've hardly said a thing.
I miss screens.

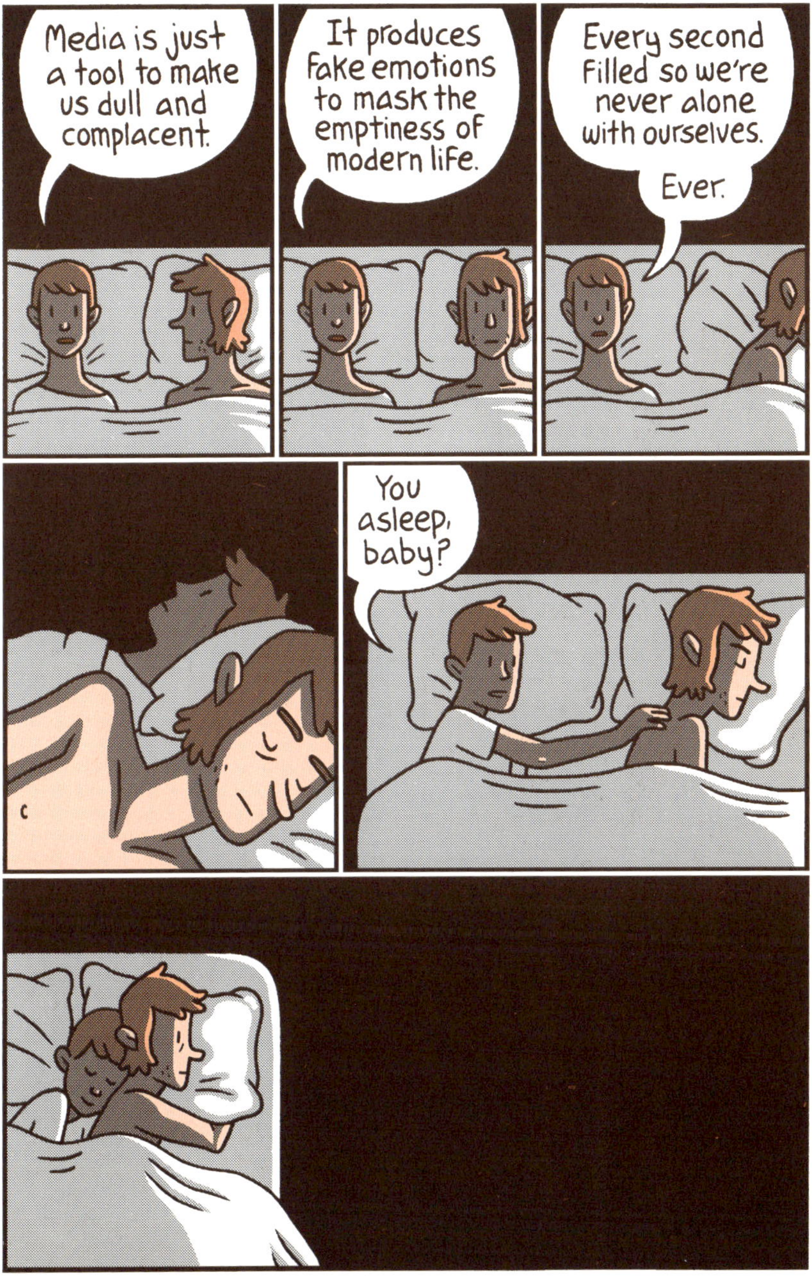
Media is just a tool to make us dull and complacent.
It produces fake emotions to mask the emptiness of modern life.
Every second filled so we're never alone with ourselves.
Ever.
You asleep, baby?

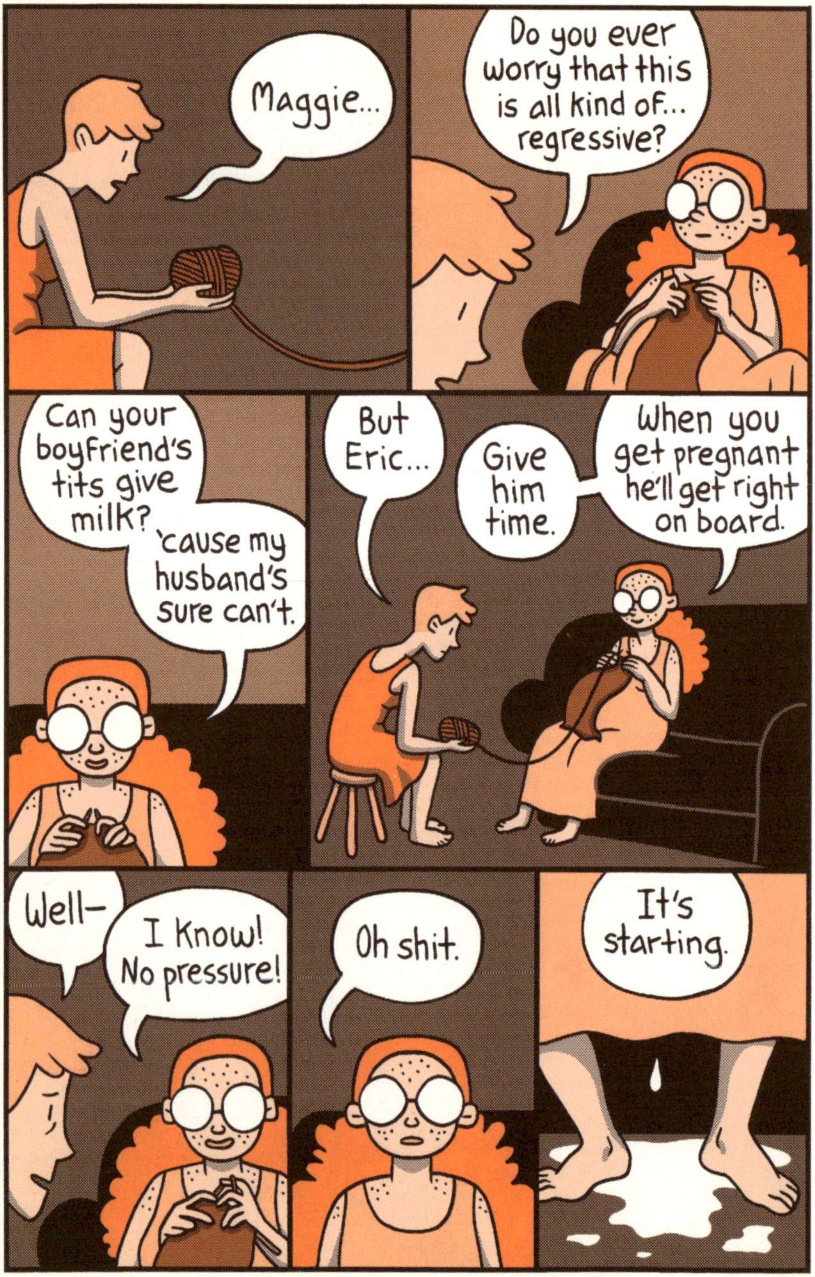
Maggie...
Do you ever worry that this is all kind of... regressive?
Can your boyfriend's tits give milk?
'cause my husband's sure can't.
But Eric...
Give him time.
When you get pregnant he'll get right on board.
Well–
I know! No pressure!
Oh shit.
It's starting.

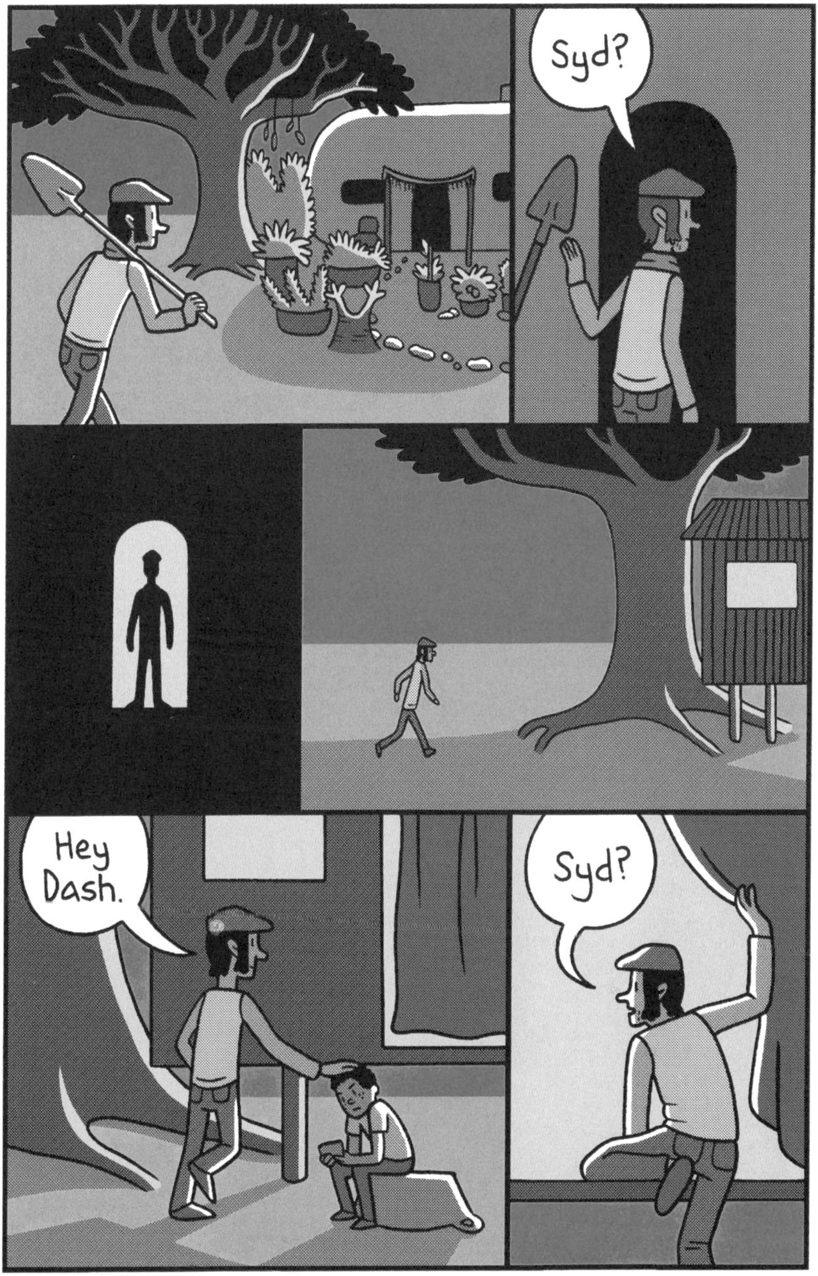
Syd?
Hey Dash.
Syd?

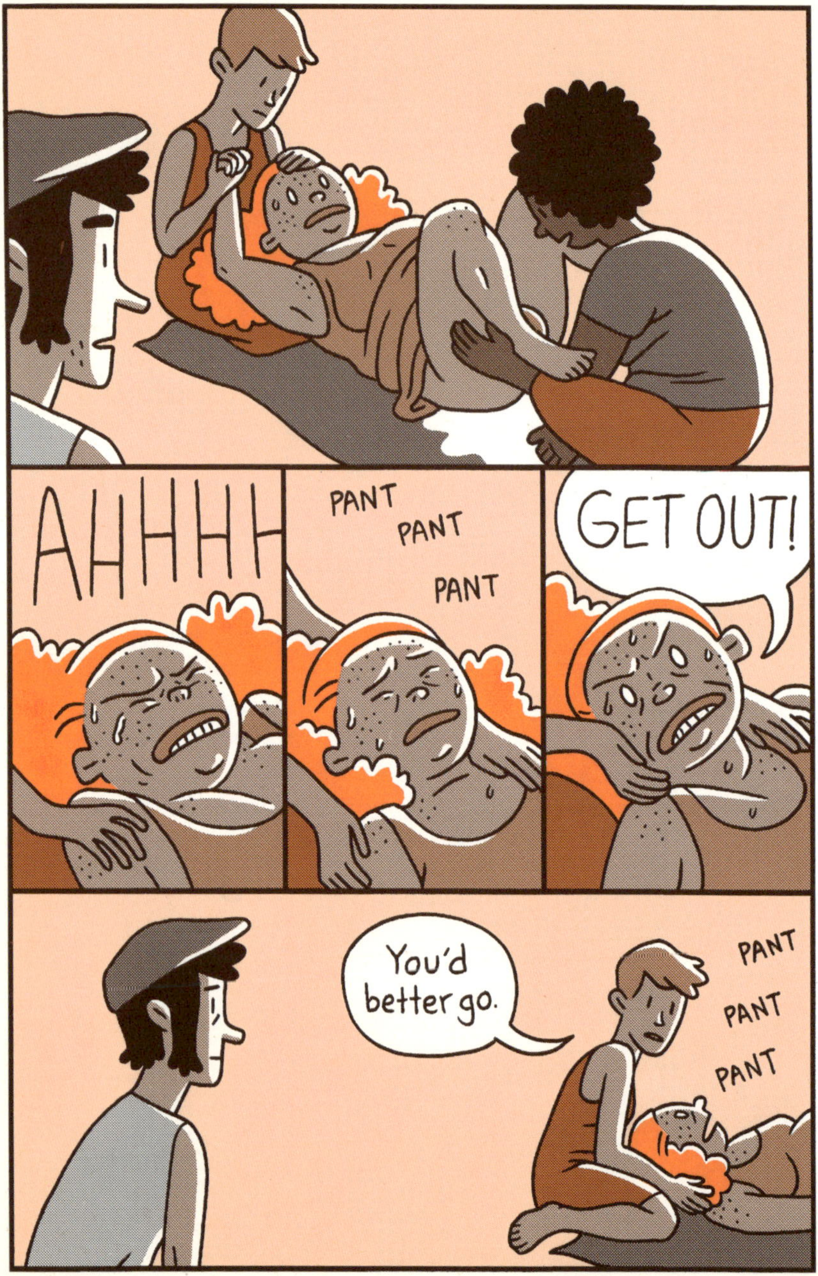
AHHHH
PANT
PANT
PANT
GET OUT!
You'd better go.
PANT
PANT
PANT

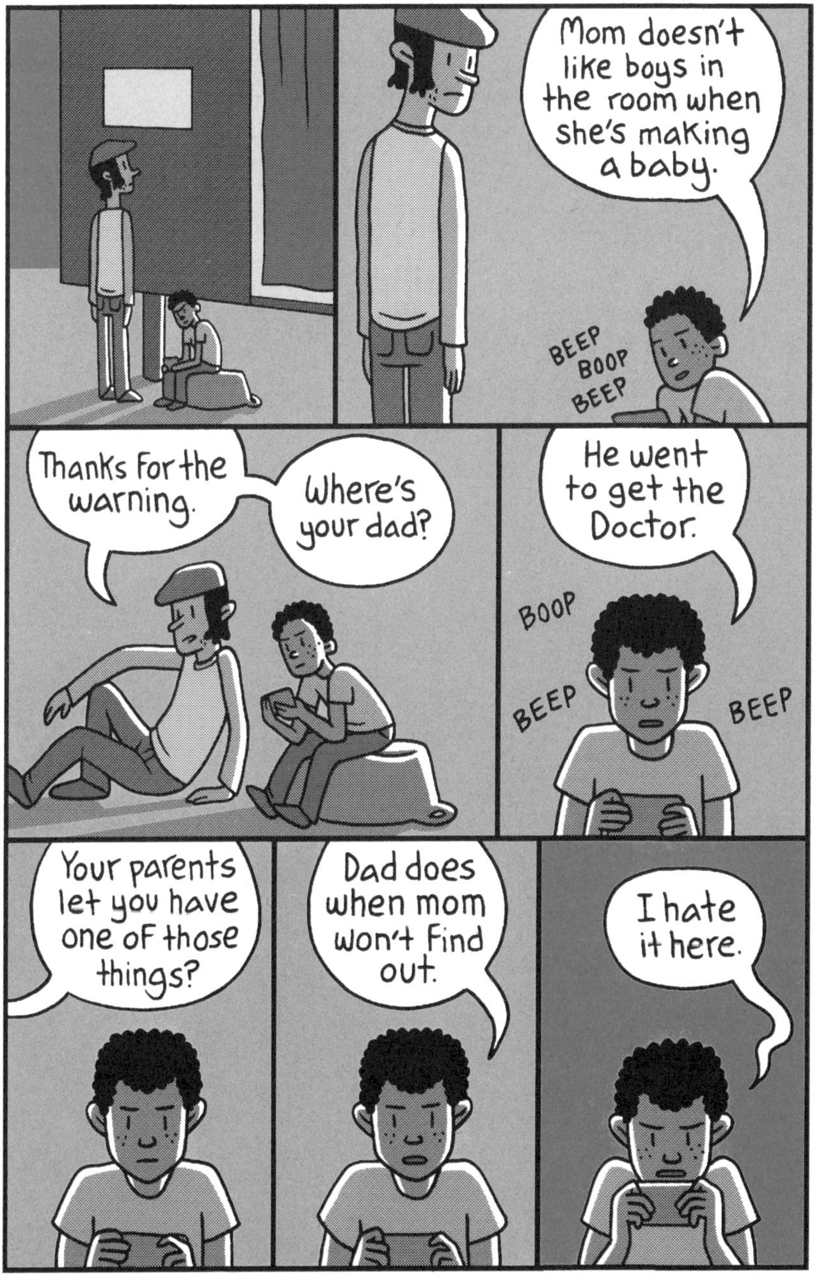
Mom doesn't like boys in the room when she's making a baby.
BEEP BOOP BEEP
Thanks for the warning.
Where's your dad?
He went to get the Doctor.
BOOP
BEEP
BEEP
Your parents let you have one of those things?
Dad does when mom won't find out.
I hate it here.

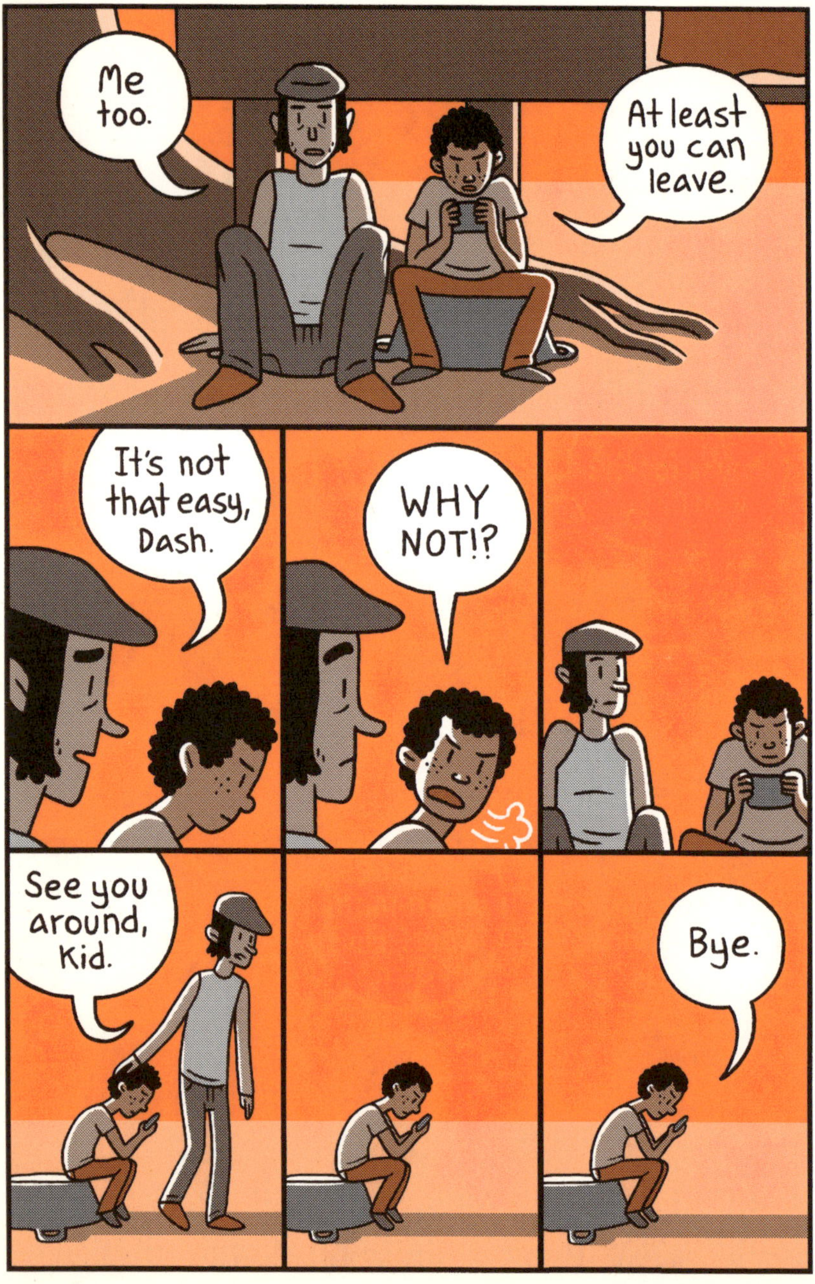
Me too.
At least you can leave.
It's not that easy, Dash.
WHY NOT!?
See you around, kid.
Bye.

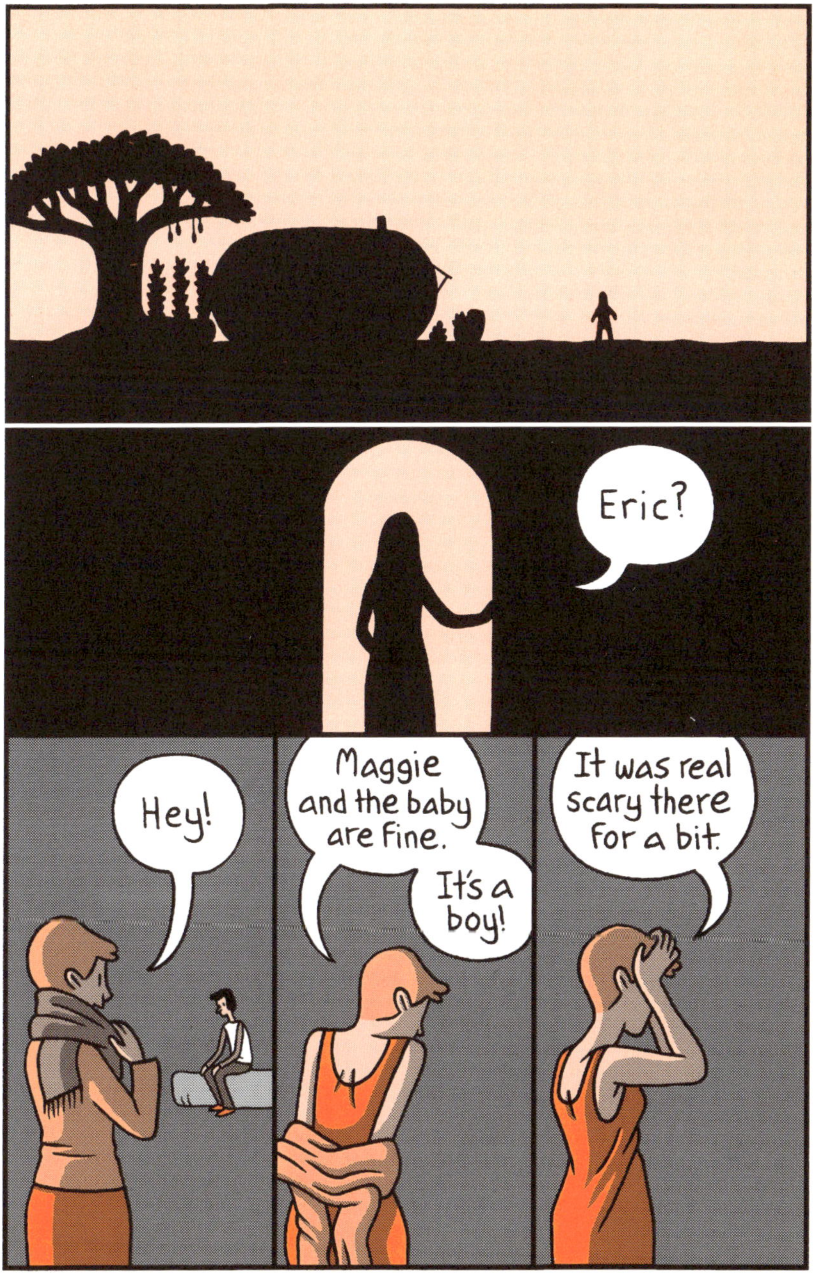
Eric?
Hey!
Maggie and the baby are fine.
It's a boy!
It was real scary there for a bit.

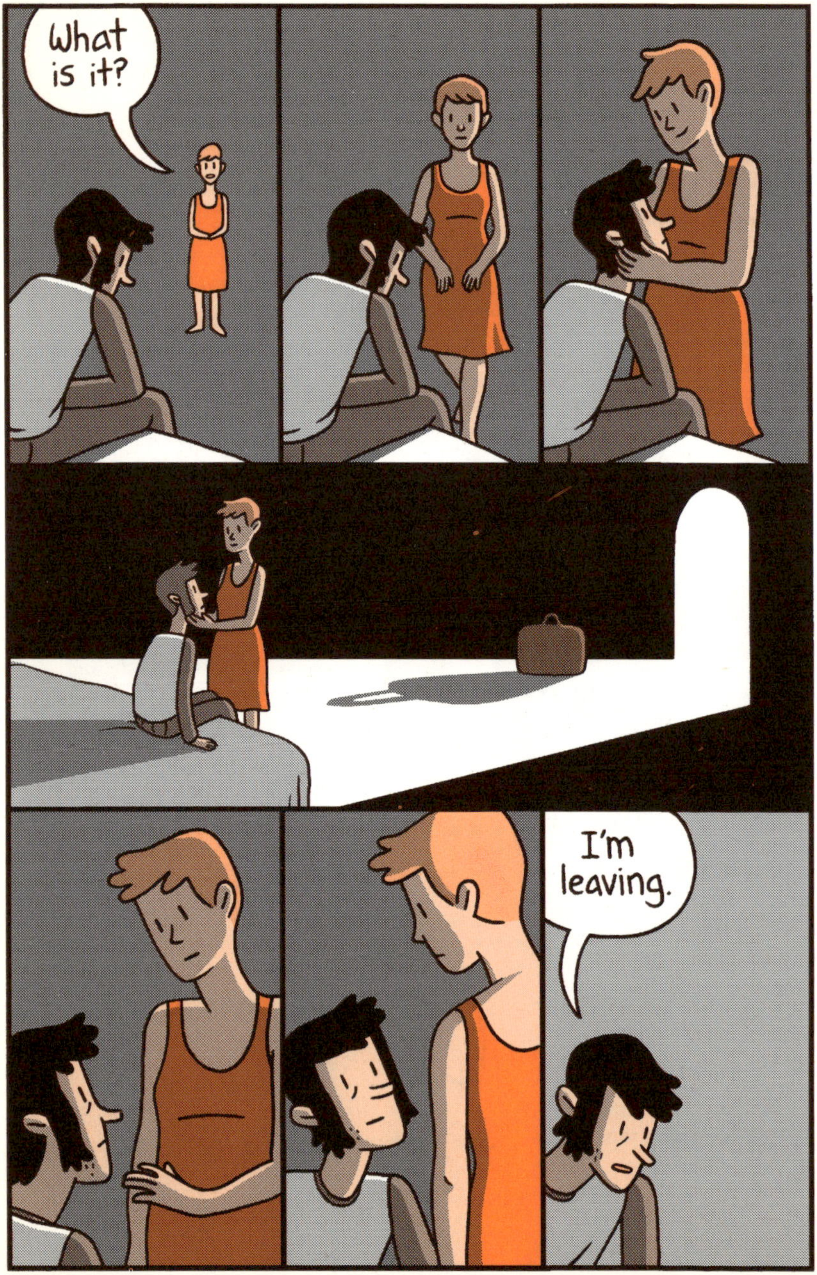
What is it?
I'm leaving.

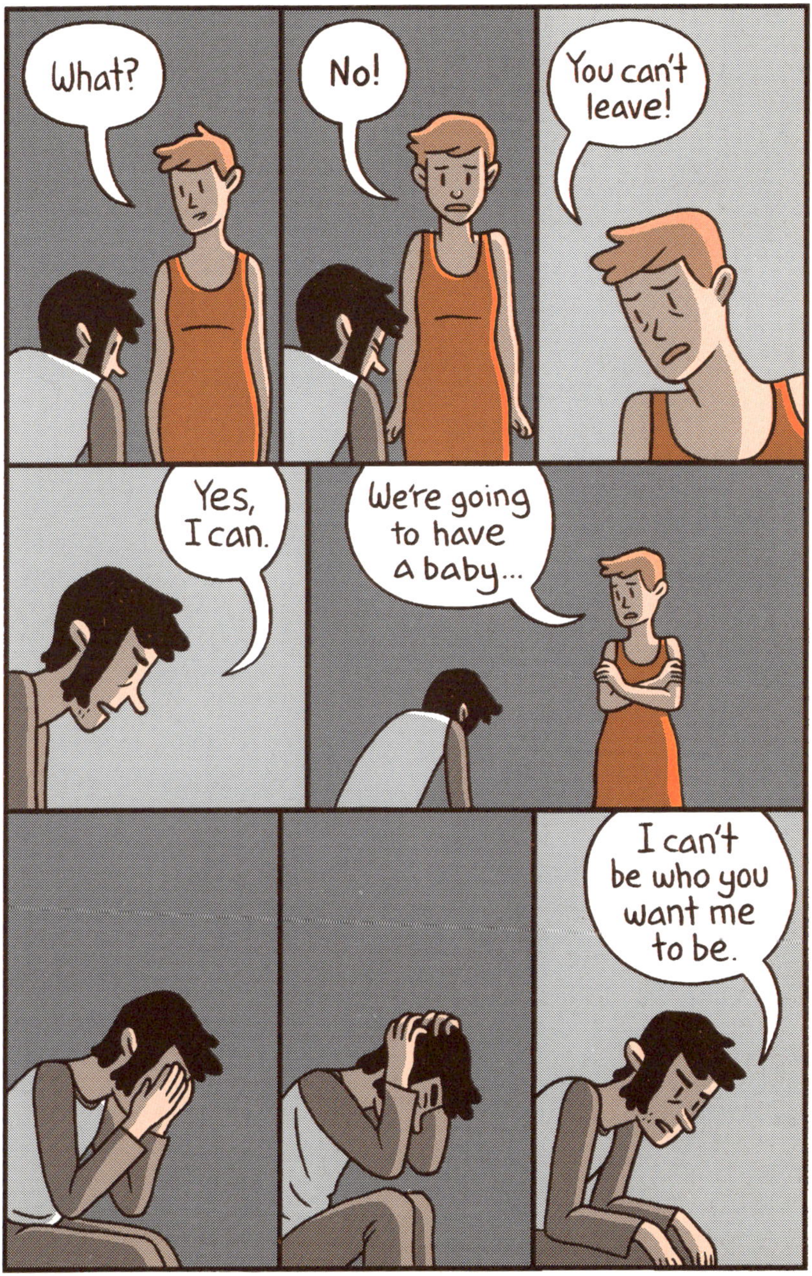
What?
No!
You can't leave!
Yes, I can.
We're going to have a baby...
I can't be who you want me to be.

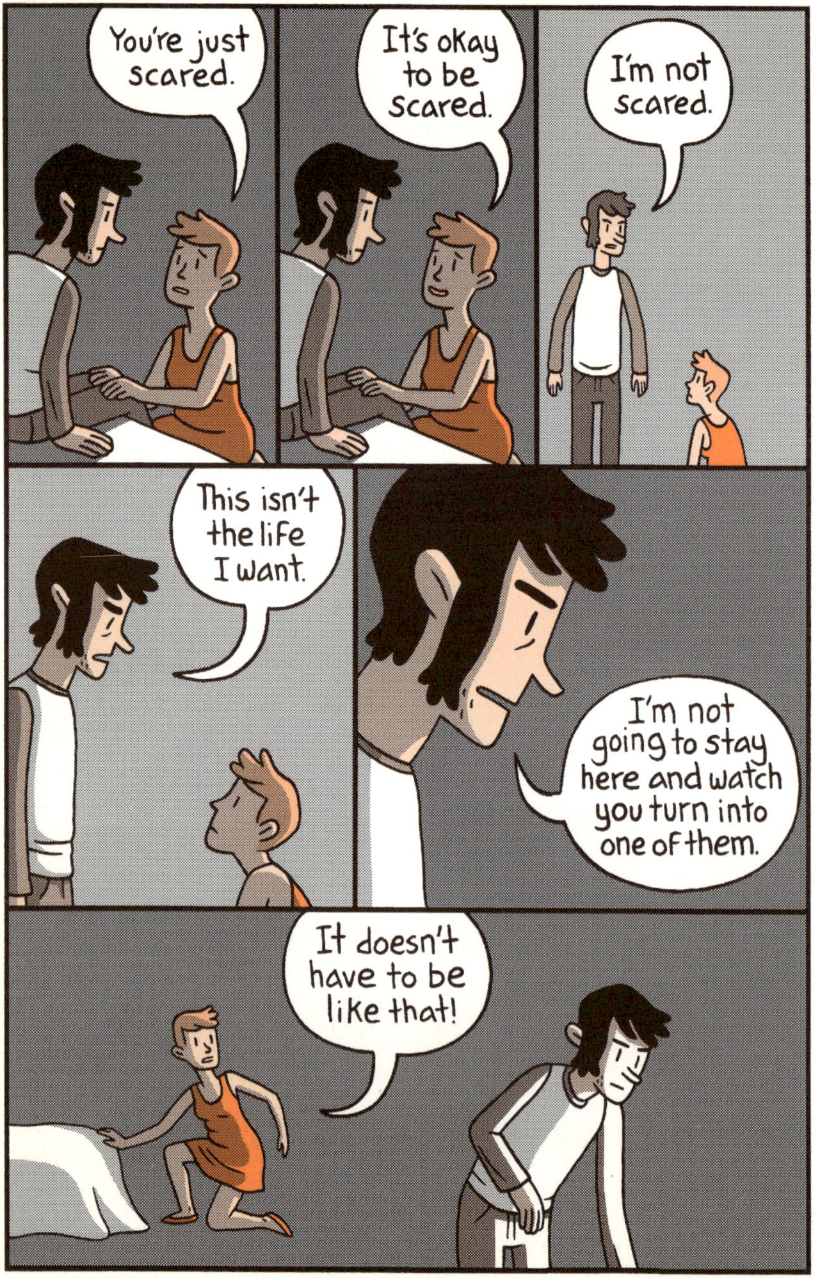
You're just scared.
It's okay to be scared.
I'm not scared.
This isn't the life I want.
I'm not going to stay here and watch you turn into one of them.
It doesn't have to be like that!

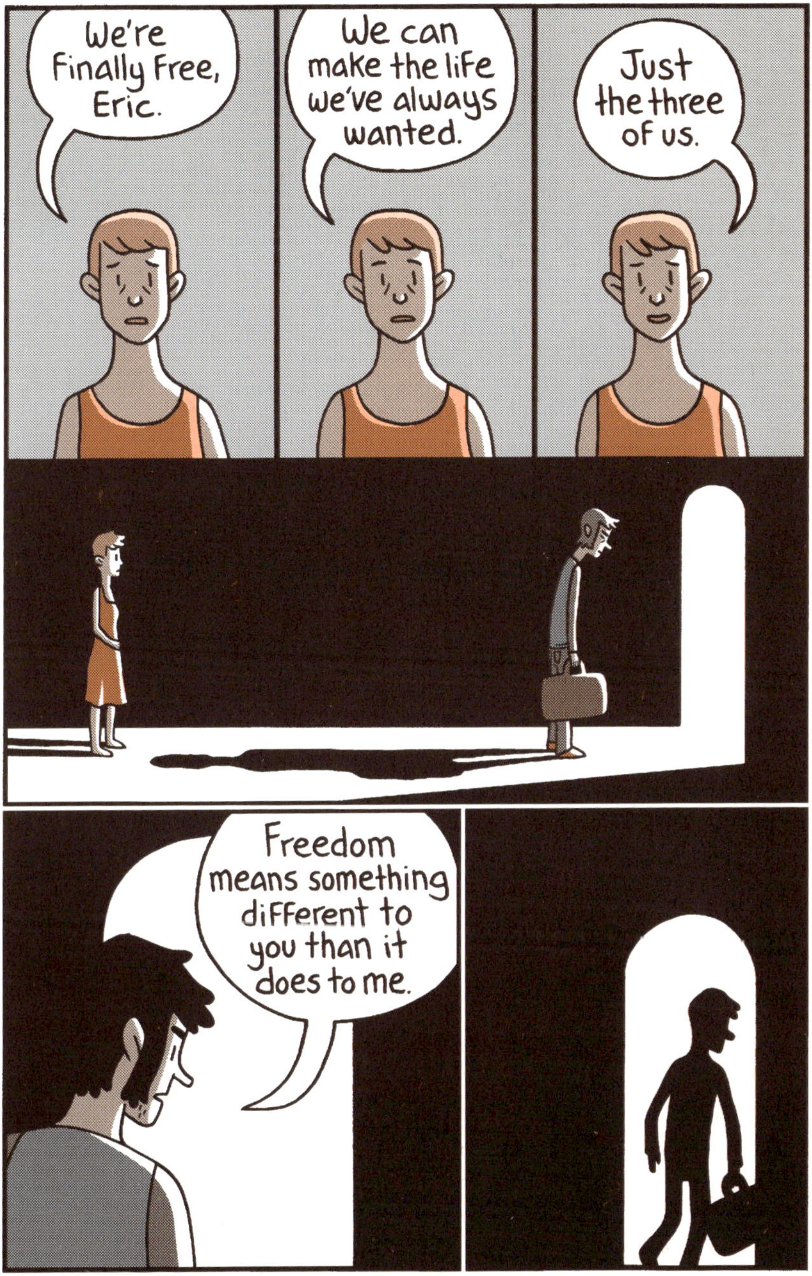
We're Finally Free, Eric.
We can make the life we've always wanted.
Just the three of us.
Freedom means something different to you than it does to me.

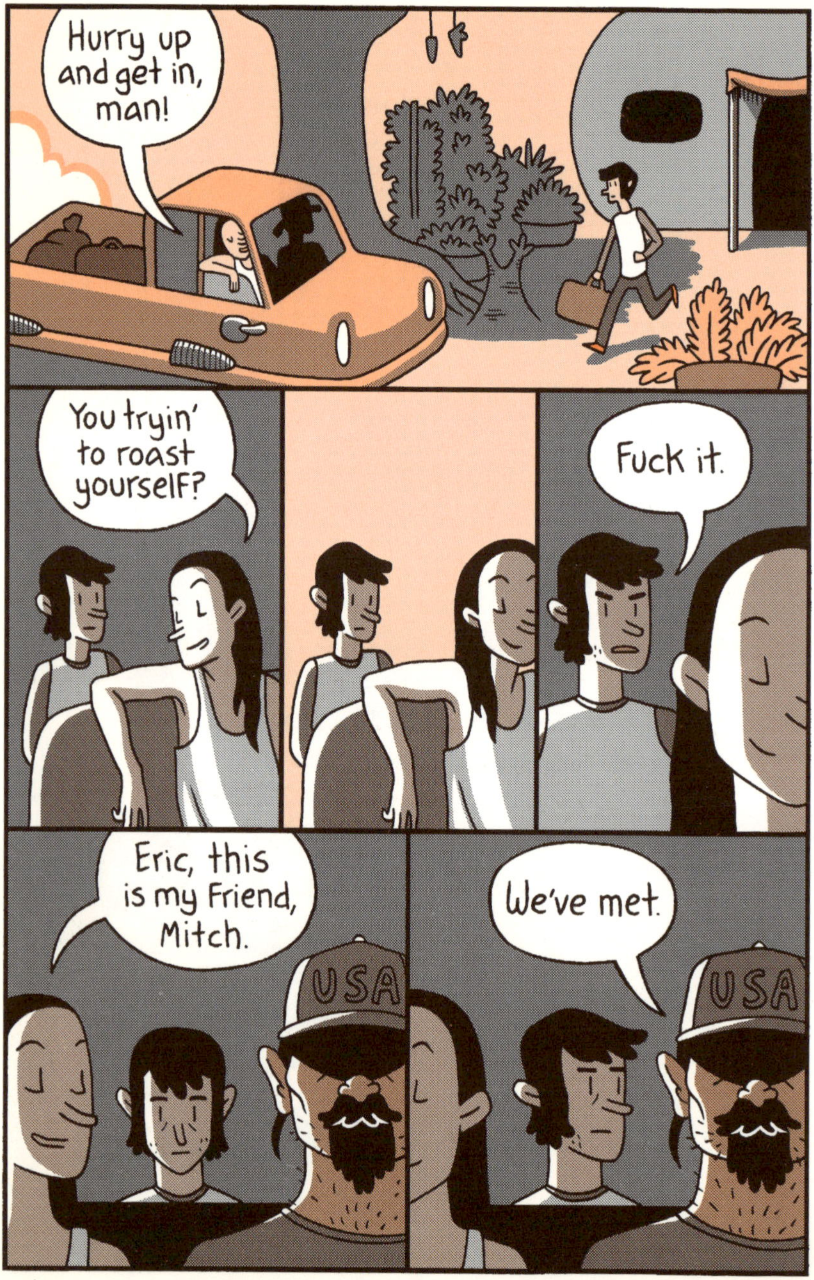
Hurry up and get in, man!
You tryin' to roast yourself?
Fuck it.
Eric, this is my Friend, Mitch.
USA
USA
We've met.

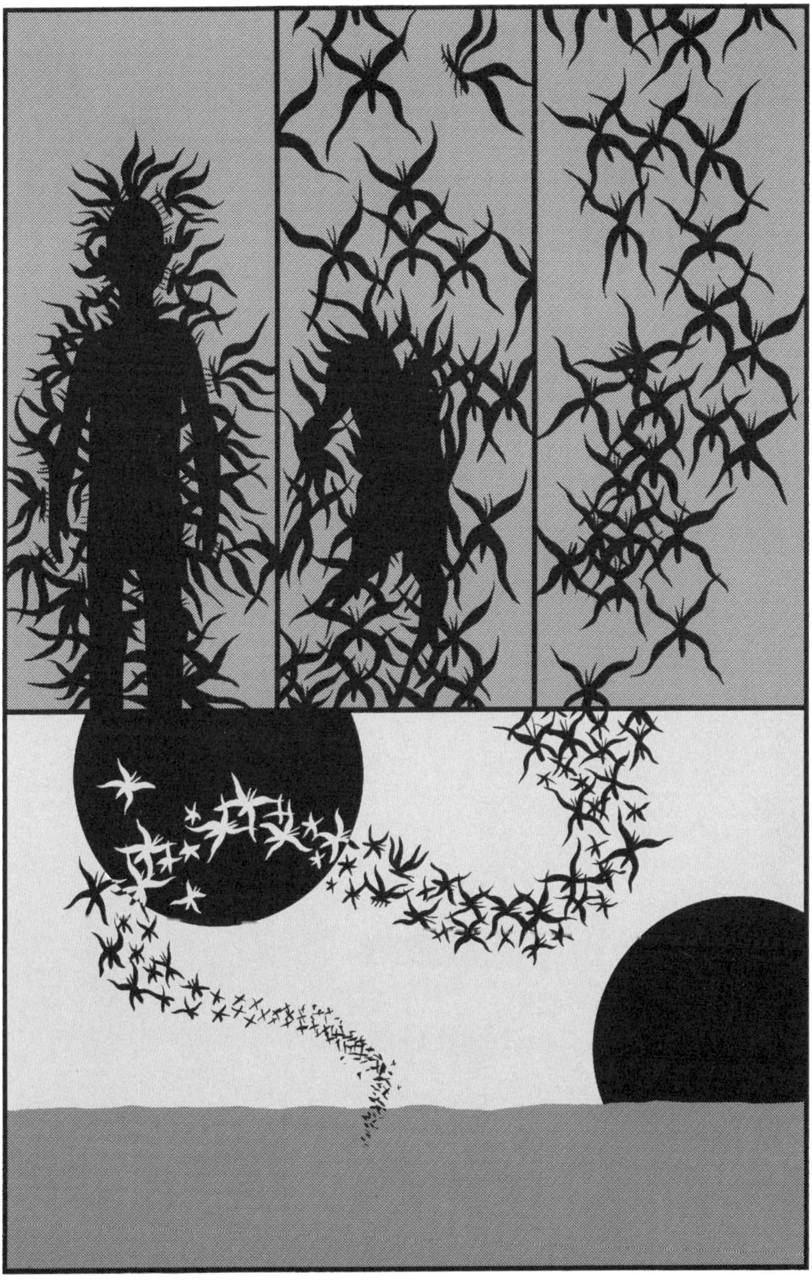

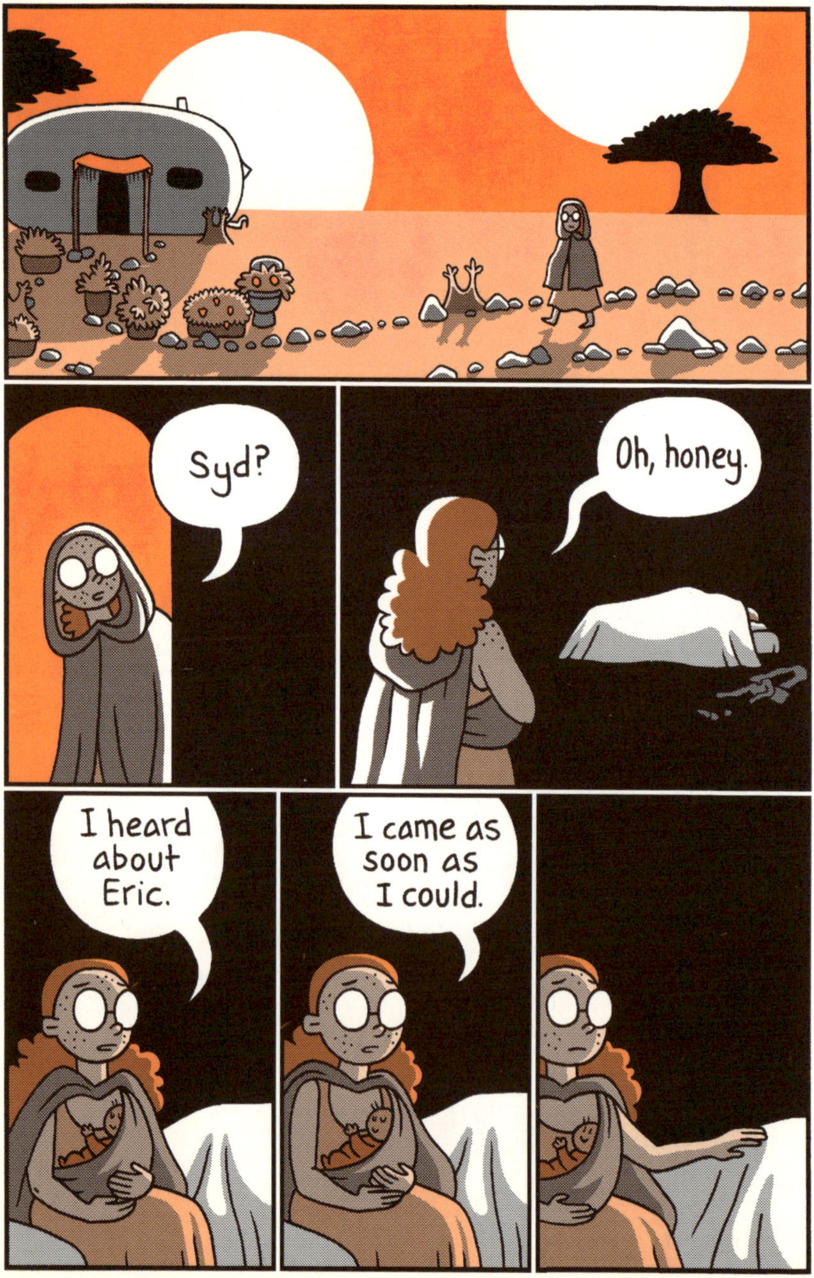
Syd?
Oh, honey.
I heard about Eric.
I came as soon as I could.

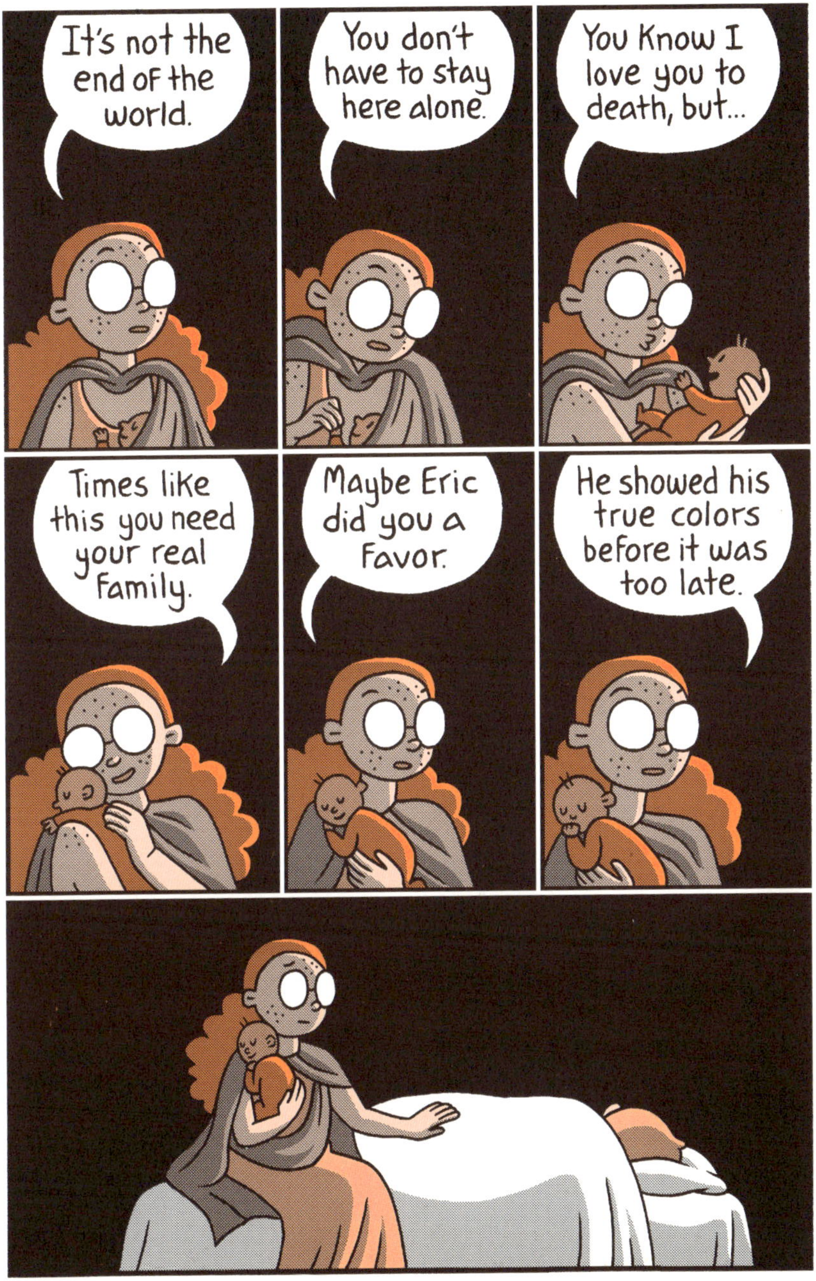
It's not the end of the world.
You don't have to stay here alone.
You Know I love you to death, but...
Times like this you need your real Family.
Maybe Eric did you a Favor.
He showed his true colors before it was too late.

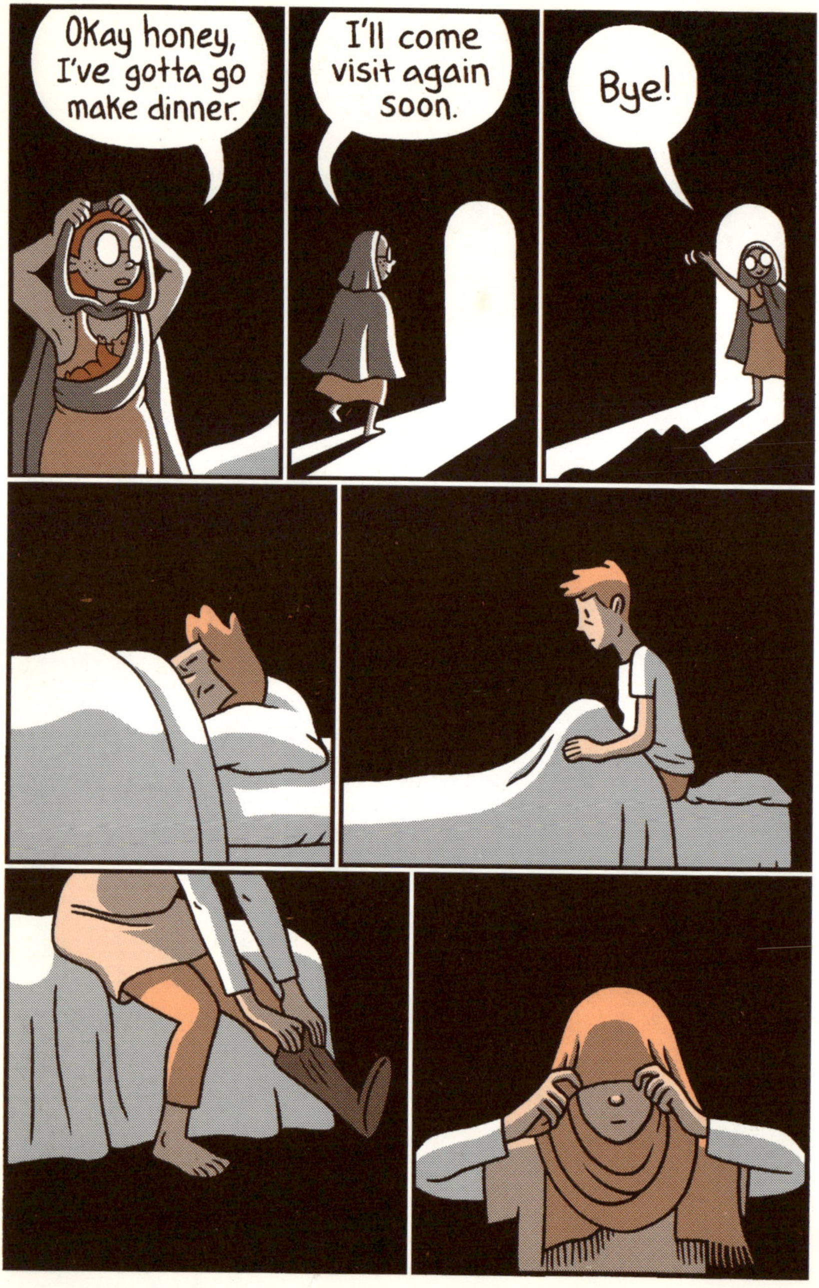
OKay honey, I've gotta go make dinner.
I'll come visit again soon.
Bye!

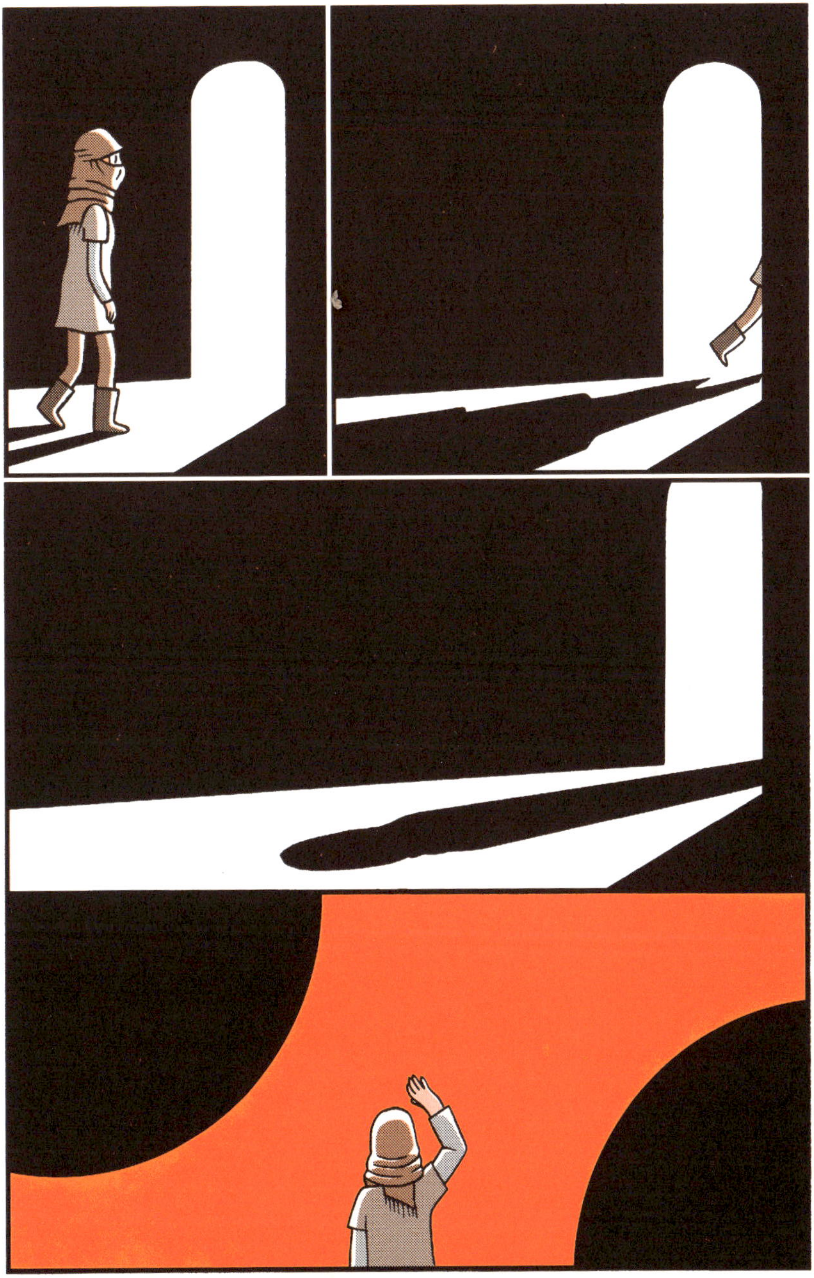

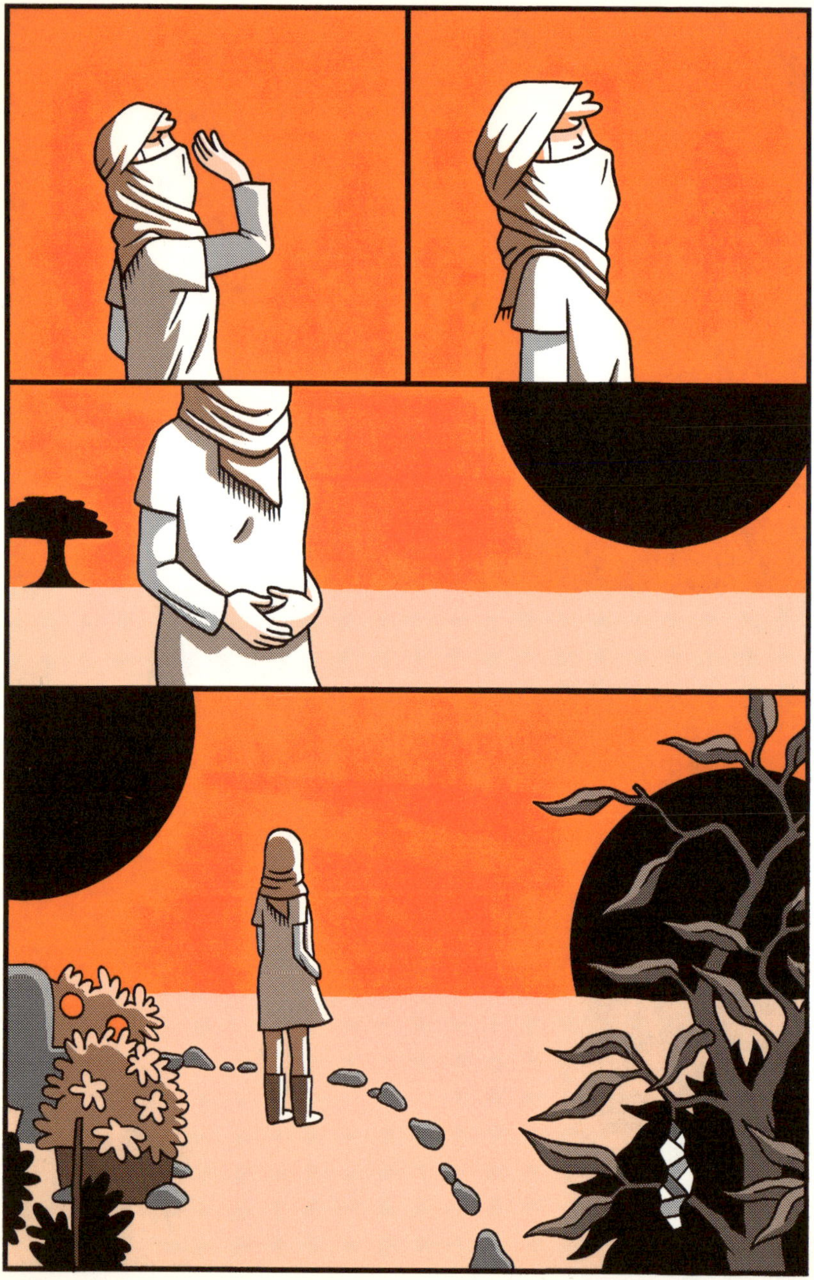

Sophie Goldstein is a 2013 graduate
of the Center for Cartoon Studies.
In 2014 she won an Ignatz Award for her
mini-comic, *House of Women, Part I*.
Her work has appeared in various
publications, including *Best American
Comics 2013, The Pitchfork Review,
Maple Key Comics, Sleep of Reason,
Symbolia, Trip 8* and *Irene 3*.

She currently lives in Pittsburgh, PA.